Southern Cyprus

by Trevor Greensmith

Reprinted 1998

' . . . out of Africa there comes always
something new . . . ' (Pliny)

'In conclusion I will now highly praise Cyprus
. . . its richness in honey, cheese . . .
copper, iron and the cotton stone . . .
its wealth of fruit and forest trees
and grapes and wine in endless quantities.'

(Barsky, 1736)

ISBN 0-900717-67-X

CONTENTS

Page

LIST OF ILLUSTRATIONS

PREFACE

Cyprus is the third largest island in the Mediterranean. It is a land of stark but superb mountain scenery, forests, fascinating coastlines and beaches, as well as a place of great geological, archaeological and historical importance. The most pertinent commodities, which it has in abundant supply, are sunshine and rock outcrops. Sunshine ensures that Cyprus is a popular holiday destination in the summer months, when daytime temperatures inland at Nicosia vary between 30-37°C and on the coast between 24-33°C. These high temperatures, only ameliorated slightly by ascending into the mountains, are not too conducive to very active geologising. The same is true for winter when it can be wet, cold and overcast occasionally. Undoubtedly the best time for such activities is in April, May, October and November. Even then, temperatures in secluded localities can be somewhat overpowering. March and April have the great advantages of having day temperatures akin to a warm English early summer and being a peak period for the blooming of a very wide variety of wild flowers, such as anemones, asphodels, rock-roses, lavender, orchids and poppies, which proliferate on the thin soils.

Almost the first thing which strikes a visitor to the island used to lush pastures is the rather bare and sparsely vegetated landscape, especially in the lowland areas. This reflects extensive de-forestation from Roman times through to the Middle Ages, but even now is exacerbated by long-established farming practices. The valleys and lower-lying ground commonly carry an intermittent, almost scrublike, plant cover, which has probably remained unaltered for many centuries. Carob, spiny burnet, gorse, thyme, myrtle and olive are common. In the more exposed and higher mountainous terrain of Troodos, where there has been much re-afforestation, these plants give way to pine, golden oak, juniper, cedar and arbutus (the red-barked strawberry tree). The general sparsity of plant cover works to the advantage of the geologically inclined and the present proliferation of rock exposures inland, and along the coast, ensures that any degree of interest in the rocks can be catered for.

This guide is to some of the more accessible rock outcrops in southern Cyprus, including those of the world famous Troodos (Troodhos) Range. It is designed to give the questing novice in the subject of Geology a glimpse of the wide variety of igneous, sedimentary and occasional metamorphic rock types, and rock structures, which constitute this sector of the island and explain the significance of what can be seen at any given locality. Nonetheless, many technical names and expressions have had to be introduced, which is why a glossary is included.

The selected localities and routes, some arranged in the form of a circular tour, are arranged in alphabetical order, each commonly including several linked rock exposures. By careful planning one or more localities can be put together to create your own personal itinerary (Figure 1). Residence in the area bounded by

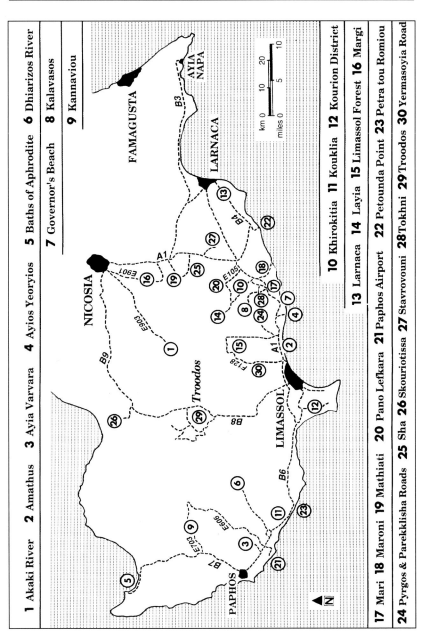

Figure 1: Itineraries map.

Preface

Nicosia, Limassol, Paphos and Polis is greatly advantageous to a successful outcome of your visit; staying at Ayia Napa involves excessive time-consuming travel. Topographical maps are essential for your planning. For example, the Bartholomew 1:300,000 Holiday Map can be bought cheaply in the U.K. and in Cyprus and is adequate when used in combination with the location maps in the Guide and suitable markers on the ground, which are identified in the text. However, they do tend to lack the degree of detail which some find desirable. The conveniently scaled 1:50,000 K717 Series, published mainly in the 1970's is currently (in 1994) out of print. It had the great advantage of having a grid for reference purposes and most of the localities mentioned in the text also carry such a reference derived from it. The newer 1:100,000 DLS Series, revised in 1991, does not carry a grid. Most of the maps do not take into account a plethora of new roads, village by-passes, road straightenings or even reservoir sites which characterise the increasing economic activity of the island. Maps, other than the holiday varieties, are available relatively cheaply, directly, but pre-paid, from the Department of Lands and Surveys, Ministry of the Interior, Nicosia. They are not readily found in book shops in the major towns of Cyprus. The Department also issues an excellent coloured 1:250,000 Geological Map of the whole island. Over the last few decades the Geological Survey Department has produced a number of 1:25,000 geology maps, of which the Akamas-Poli area (Sheet 8 III, IV) and Southern Troodos Transform Fault Zone (Limassol Forest) (Sheet 2) are prime examples, though cover is incomplete. Outside Cyprus, specialist map shops carrying a certain amount of stock include Stanfords, 12-14 Long Acre, London WC2E 9LP and Map Link, 25 East Mason Street, Santa Barbara, California 93101.

Since 1991, and especially evident on the road signs on main roads, there has been put into effect standardisation of the spelling of geographical names. Thus, Ayia and Ayios on tourist and other maps now read Agia and Agios on the signs, Larnaca now becomes Larnaka, Akrounda becomes Akrounta, Parekklisha becomes Parekklisia, Yermasoyia becomes Germasogeia, Khirokitia becomes Choirokoitia, Limassol becomes Lemesos, Nicosia becomes Lefkosia, and so on. These changes create no problems for the visitor. A very useful asset in location finding are the recently emplaced white roadside kilometre pegs.

Undoubtedly, the best method of making the most of the time available on the island is to hire a vehicle from one of the numerous firms scattered throughout all the major holiday centres. There are no trains in Cyprus. The bus services, though they connect with most villages, run at inconvenient times and/or infrequently. Taxis are used a lot by visitors, but over a period they can prove expensive. The major roads are metalled and the connections between Nicosia, Larnaca and Limassol are up to motorway standards. However, the metalled roads leading to some of the localities in this guide often rapidly deteriorate into hard packed earth, which is susceptible to deterioration and can be very slippery after a wet spell. Consequently, the ideal vehicle to hire is a 4-wheel drive type. Driving is on the left. In the country, petrol stations are sparse and on Sundays and Public Holidays are either closed or in the 24 Hour self-service category with an ingenious, but simple, system of payment. It is probably better to make sure you fill-up beforehand if travelling any distance on these or any other days.

Apart from wearing sensible footwear and clothing appropriate to the prevailing weather conditions, and possibly carrying a small magnifying hand-lens (x7), there is no need for any special geological equipment. Loose collectable material is invariably present at all localities, so hammering is totally unnecessary and indeed is undesirable. Under no circumstances must archaeological material be displaced or removed from any site. It is illegal to do so. The local inhabitants are very friendly and it is courteous to them, and appreciated, if no damage is done to rock outcrops or adjacent growing crops. In the warmth of spring and autumn keep an eye out for snakes, especially one stubby, mottled viper with a yellow horn-like tail, called koufi locally.

The Cyprus Tourism Organisation is a fount of information on all aspects of the island, producing a wide range of tourist maps, pamphlets, handbooks and bus time-tables designed to help you in your stay. There are offices in all the main holiday centres. In the U.K. the Cyprus Tourism Office address is 213 Regent Street, London W1R 8DA (Tel. 071 734 9822).

This Guide has been written with the amateur geologist totally in mind and is based on nearly ten years of personal excursioning to the island, usually with a party of undergraduates in tow. It draws heavily on information published in several specialist Ophiolite Symposia and other Field Guides, and the vast literature, but also incorporates the knowledge of members of the Cyprus Geological Survey Department, more especially Costas Xenophontos, and of various colleagues, Adrian Jones, Roger Mason and Wendy Kirk, in the Department of Geological Sciences at University College London. However, the author is solely responsible for any misinterpretations, or interpretations differing from the 'official line', in attempting to simplify for the casual visitor what is a very complicated story. I am also very grateful to the Geologists' Association for financially supporting this enterprise. The line drawings were compiled by Colin Stuart and the plates made by Michael Gray both at University College London. This Guide has benefited considerably from the acute critical eye of my wife, a trained geologist, who edited the text, word processed it into a manageable form, and was ever conscious of the principle that this was an instructional as well as a purely informational text.

THE GEOLOGICAL FRAMEWORK OF CYPRUS

The geology of Cyprus is a subject of unending controversy for countless geologists and has been so for many decades. Distilling the essence out of the various and often contradictory arguments put forward in the now extensive scientific literature is akin to exercising the Judgement of Solomon. Most of the detailed petrological and tectonic work has been on the remarkably well-exposed and world-famous ophiolite (igneous) complex, which outcrops in the Troodos mountains and adjacent Limassol Forest area, so this complex will be described in some detail.

In simple terms, Cyprus is presently located in an actively unstable zone between two major plate-like masses. To the south and southwest is the African Plate, which since early Mesozoic times has been moving relative to a northern mass, known as the Eurasian Plate. A much smaller mobile plate, the Arabian Plate, impinges against both in the vicinity of the Dead Sea and Red Sea. The island and its immediate surrounds appear to be a segment of oceanic crust and mantle separated from the edge of one of the two major plates by rift-faulting, possibly during Triassic times (about 230 million years ago). The segment, or microplate, now consists in part of the Troodos ophiolite, for which there is indirect geomagnetic evidence of its initiation during the middle of Cretaceous times (about 95 million years ago) and which formed during a phase of constructive growth (spreading) of the sea-floor. (Although sometimes referred to as the Turkey or Anatolian Plate this Guide adopts, for convenience, the non-technical, informal term 'Cyprus Microplate'; it has no status in the literature).

The manner of movement of the adjacent plates at and since those times has varied considerably. Sometimes they have moved directly and destructively against each other by processes known as obduction and subduction, and one or other was over-ridden. At other times they moved laterally past each other by processes known as strike-slip and transform faulting. Such faulting commonly precedes phases of upthrusting (obduction) of oceanic crust. Many authorities believe that the spreading phase, during which the ophiolite was generated, coincided with a major phase of subduction of the African Plate beneath the 'Cyprus Microplate'. They describe the situation as supra-subduction spreading. At a later obduction stage the ophiolite was thrust upwards in form of a slab detached from its roots, coming to rest on continental crust. The combination and sequence of these events has meant that both the ophiolite, which forms the foundation of the whole of the island (with some extensions offshore), and some of the overlying associated sediments have been laterally moved from their original position to where we now see them. It is estimated that there has been a migration or drift northwards of some 10-15° latitude and a 90° counter-clockwise rotation since Cretaceous times. Some workers suggest that the rotation only started in Upper Miocene times, but this view is strongly resisted by others who favour rotation commencing in late Cretaceous times. These movements have ensured that the island and its surrounds have remained unstable through to the present day with recurrent uplift and faulting. This has been partly expressed by earth tremors, some reaching a magnitude of 6 or greater on the Richter Scale and deeply focussed, associated with a major dislocation or subduction zone running east-west and probably located 50km to the south of the island. The Paphos area seems to have been most affected over the more recent centuries with major tremors in 15 B.C., which led to the total destruction of Old Paphos, and in A.D.17, 332, 1189 and 1953.

In general, the sea water depth in the Cyprus region has diminished progressively since Cretaceous times and a land area of some sort has existed on the present site of the island from Middle Miocene times onwards.

The island as a whole is broadly divisible into 4 topographical areas, each having an east-west, mildly arcuate trend. The topography reflects the underlying geology to a remarkable degree (Figure 2 and Table 1).

Extending along the full northern length is the Kyrenia Range, 3-10km in width and rising to about 1000m above sea-level, and resonant with castellated Lusignan ruins (A.D. 1192-1489), such as at Buffavento. Overlooking and dominating Nicosia and its outskirts are craggy, upstanding outcrops, including Pentadactylos ('five-fingers') Mountain, rising to 749m and described as looking like a mailed fist. Unfortunately, the rocks and ancient ruins of the range, so tantalisingly visible, are difficult to get to from southern Cyprus and are not included in this Guide. In brief, the spine of the range comprises a basal series of Permo-Carboniferous limestones, succeeded by Triassic and Jurassic limestones, commonly recrystallised to dolomites and marbles, and brecciated, Cretaceous limestones and chalks interbedded with basic pillow lavas and rhyolitic volcanic deposits, these being followed by Palaeocene to Eocene limestones, chalks and marls. All these beds were subject to powerful compressive earth-movements, more especially in Oligocene and late Miocene times, and expressed by major E-W and north-dipping tectonic slices. Small outcrops of low-grade metamorphic rocks, of doubtful age, appear to have been caught up in these displacements. Some workers believe that lateral strike-slip movements along the faults were important at these times of marked tectonism. The thick sequences of Oligocene and Miocene breccias, sandstones and chalky marls, some carrying olistoliths of older rocks, flanking the core of the range reflect a significant change in depositional conditions during the later stages of the tectonism. This trend continued through to Plio-Pleistocene times which saw, eventually, the final emergence of the range above sea-level and passage into a continuing regime of sub-aerial denudation.

To the immediate south of the Kyrenia Range and to the east of Nicosia is the gently rolling low-lying Mesaoria Plain, the cradle of the Cypriot Mycenaean culture from 1400 B.C., and until recently the 'breadbasket' of the island. It is underlain at depth by a northwards extension of the Troodos ophiolite pillow lavas on which rests a succession of Upper Cretaceous to Quaternary

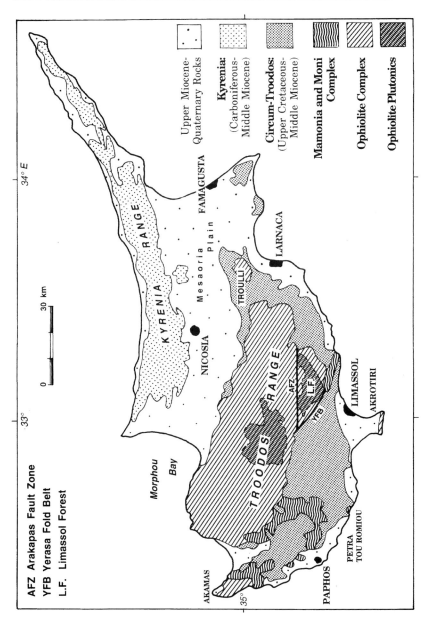

Figure 2: Geological map of Cyprus (simplified, after the Cyprus Geological Survey, Robertson and others).

		Table 1	
		SIMPLIFIED GEOLOGICAL SUCCESSION (SW CYPRUS)	
	Holocene		Alluvium, beach barriers, caliche.
QUATERNARY	Pleistocene		Raised beaches & river terraces. Fanglomerates.
		Athalassa Fm (0-40m)	Sands & marls.
	Pliocene	Nicosia Fm (0-800m)	Marls.
	Miocene	Kalavasos Fm (0-150m) & Koronia Mem (0-150m)	Evaporites. Limestones, Patch reefs.
NEOGENE (Tertiary)		Pakhna Fm (0-700m)	Marls, sandstones & conglomerates.
		Terra Mem (0-100m)	Limestones.
	Oligocene	U. Lefkara Fm (0-200m)	Marls.
PALAEOGENE (Tertiary)	Eocene & Palaeocene	M. Lefkara Fm (0-450m)	Chalks, marls & cherts.
	Late Cretaceous	L. Lefkara Fm (0-75m) (Maastrichtian)	Marls, chalks.
		MAMONIA COMPLEX (Maastrichtian)	Moni & Kathikas melanges. Ayios Photios & Dhiarizos Groups.
MESOZOIC		Kannaviou Fm (0-650m) (Maastrichtian & Campanian)	Volcaniclastic sandstones & bentonitic clays.
		Perapedhi Fm (0-55m) (Campanian)	Radiolarite muds, & umbers.
	Cretaceous	TROODOS OPHIOLITE	(See Fig. 3)

sedimentary rocks, several thousands of metres in thickness. Beneath Morphou Bay geophysical studies indicate a thickness of 5300m. The late Cretaceous and Tertiary beds, deposited in what was probably a fault-bounded, graben-like depression, comprise chalk, marl, calcareous sandstone and occasional thick Miocene salt successions (200m near to Morphou). In the northern part of the plain abutting the Kyrenia Range, the strata, especially the Middle Miocene, are highly folded giving a characteristic hummocky topography. This part is separated from the more central and southern parts by a major fault zone, the Ovgos Fault, which runs east-west beneath Nicosia. South of this fault the beds are generally little deformed.

Above these Cretaceous and Tertiary beds there are great spreads of Pleistocene gravels, sands and silts, laid down in the form of cone-like fans. These materials were generated during a major upheaval of the Troodos Range in Pleistocene times, partly caused by the serpentinisation of its core rocks. Some material also emanated from the Kyrenia Range. Subaerial erosion was profound and prolonged in the wetter periods of those times, and debris was transported considerable distances, even into the adjacent sea.

The Troodos mountain range, said to be the stronghold of Byzantium from A.D. 33-1191, looms darkly over the Mesaoria Plain and low-lying foothills to the south and southwest of Cyprus, rising in its craggy forested eminences to a height of 1920m at Mount Olympus. The bulk of the range is formed of a displaced slab of altered ultrabasic and basic plutonic igneous rocks capped by intermediate and basic lava flows (Figure 3). The rock assemblage is referred to as an ophiolite and is between 11-20km thick. Similar rocks occur in the Limassol Forest area and as inliers on the Akamas Peninsula and at Troulli, near Larnaca. The ophiolites are believed to have formed in a zone of Cretaceous sea-floor spreading about 95-80 million years ago. The parent magma was almost certainly of a low-silica, ultrabasic kind derived from the Earth's peridotite upper mantle. There was great excitement in the geological world when this mode of origin for ophiolites was deduced and this is the main reason for the great interest in Cyprus. Very few ophiolites are as easily accessible for study.

Structurally, the Troodos ophiolite now appears as an upthrust (obducted) slice of oceanic crust and uppermost mantle, predominantly displaced in late Cretaceous times soon after its generation on the ocean floor had ceased. The rocks on land are disposed at present in an east-west elongated dome resulting from subsequent periods of displacement and uplift, especially during later Tertiary and Pleistocene times. The uplift was caused in part by the generation and upwards movement of low density serpentinite masses formed by the hydrothermal alteration of deep-seated ultrabasic igneous rocks, such as harzburgites, and in part by the underthrusting of the African Plate from the south and west. The stripping off of the upper igneous levels of the ophiolite during at least the last 1.6 million years has now revealed a major proportion of its internal succession in a series of roughly concentric zones (Figure 2) (Itinerary 29). In detail the succession is quite complex with a mantle sequence succeeded by a crustal sequence and both intruded by several suites of plutonic rocks. There is also a high degree of faulting within the ophiolite often extending into and affecting the adjacent sedimentary successions. Some of the most important faulting occurs along the southern edge, where there is evidence of

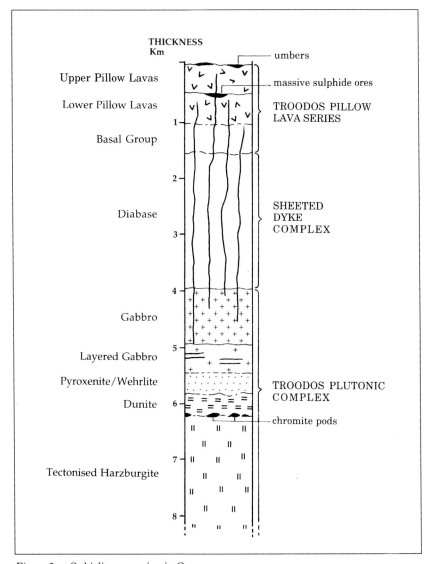

Figure 3: Ophiolite succession in Cyprus.

southwards-directed thrust fault movements, mainly occurring during later Miocene times. Miocene times, in fact, seem to have been a crucial period in the structural evolution, and possible further obduction, of the ophiolite as it has been inferred that a major, if not *the* major, phase in the ultimately 90° anticlockwise rotation of the mass with its surrounding sedimentary envelope occurred then.

The axial zone, where the mantle sequence part of the ophiolite succession is exposed, is well seen around the Troodos summit. The main rock types are harzburgites, named after the type locality near Harzburg in Germany, and altered (serpentinized) harzburgites. As befits its slow cooling history from magma generated at temperatures of 1000-1200° Centigrade and its mantle source at a depth of 50-70km, the fresh harzburgite rock is medium to coarse grained, carrying a mixture of 80 per cent or more of olivine, with orthopyroxene (enstatite). The green olivine is particularly prone to hydration (addition of water) and subsequent alteration into serpentine minerals, so that the rock has been converted over large areas into serpentinite masses, mainly intrusive in character, especially in zones of contemporaneous faulting and fracturing. These zones appear to have allowed vast volumes of sea water to penetrate to great depths in the hot ophiolite mass and bring about the conversion. Harzburgite attracts much attention because it is thought to be close in composition to the rocks forming the upper levels of the Earth's mantle. None of the other rocks in the Complex are quite like it. A noticeable feature of it in places (though also found in adjacent rocks) is a near-vertical alignment or banding of the grains, creating a linear texture or foliation. This is a secondary fabric, probably formed during a late phase of flowage of the harzburgite, when under considerable earth stresses. 'Tectonised harzburgite' is how the rock is described in the literature.

Towards the top of the harzburgite occur pods of dunite, a medium to coarse grained, essentially mono-mineralic rock composed of olivine. These pods increase in size and number upwards and eventually form major discontinuous intrusive bodies, up to a kilometre wide and outcropping over a distance of 18km on the north, west and south flanks of Mount Olympus. They carry small chromite bodies adjacent to contacts with the harzburgites. Associated with these rocks are other plutonic rocks composed mainly of pyroxenes (pyroxenites), a mixture of clinopyroxenes and olivines (wehrlites), or a mixture of plagioclase feldspars and pyroxenes (gabbros).

The crustal sequence forms the top part of the ophiolite and comprises a range of essentially basic rocks including intrusives, such as peridotite and gabbro, and extrusives, such as basalt. The main gabbro outcrops surround the ultrabasic rocks of the axial zone and at certain levels a distinct near-horizontal layering is present, suggestive of plastic flow in magma chambers. The upper parts of the gabbro masses are often intruded by discontinuous bodies and dykes of creamy coloured plagiogranite, a mixture of plagioclase feldspar and quartz, with a sprinkling of ferro-magnesian silicates.

The greater part of the Troodos Range is formed of the Sheeted Dyke Complex (or Diabase Group), and this is well-exposed on the flanks of the core rocks. The outcrops are characterised by a very angular, craggy topography which relates to the disposition of the rocks, which is in the form of a huge number of closely-packed, usually near-vertical, altered mainly doleritic dykes, with some others of micro-dioritic and epidosite (epidote, feldspar, quartz and amphibole) constitution. Diabase is the name commonly applied to altered dolerites. Because of the type of hydrothermal alteration or metamorphism to which they have been subject, caused by the activities of invasive sea waters at temperatures of 200-400°C, all the rocks in the Diabase Group belong to what is technically known as the 'green schist facies'.

The dykes appear to have been emplaced by the infilling of tension fractures rather than by forceful injection. Each dyke may vary in thickness from a few centimetres to about 5 metres although most are less than 2 metres wide. Their orientation is variable, though in some areas there is a marked north-south or northwest-southeast trend (Itinerary 27). At some lower levels in the Complex the dyke density is very high, approaching 100 per cent; this makes it difficult to determine the nature of the host rock. This density implies a 100 per cent extension of the crust. The only satisfactory mechanism to account for such extension is sea-floor spreading. In general, the thin 'screens' of host rock are mainly altered lavas and gabbros, now containing epidote.

Above the Sheeted Dyke Complex, in the Basal Group of the Pillow Lava succession, the dykes are less densely concentrated and the host rocks are mainly heavily chloritised pillow lavas. Some probably acted as feeders for the lava flows. All of these rocks are very actively worked for aggregates and other industrial purposes.

The Basal Group is capped by a sequence of fine grained, mildly metamorphosed lavas and extrusive breccias, which outcrop in a discontinuous lower-lying belt around the margins of the Troodos Range (Itineraries 1 and 16). Technically they belong to the 'zeolite facies', reflecting hydrothermal metamorphism at temperatures between 100-200°C. The most extensive outcrop is in the east in the Sha-Mathiati area, where it is between 6-15km wide. The thickness of the lava pile, which poured out onto a very irregular sea bottom is very difficult to estimate and varies from locality to locality, but probably totalled about 1.5km. It is usual practice to separate the pile into a Lower Pillow Lava and Upper Pillow Lava series though, in reality, it is not easy to locate the boundary between the two. In some areas to the north-centre and to the south of Troodos there is evidence for unconformity between them. It seems likely from their chemistry that the Lower Lavas were erupted near to active spreading axes or centres, whereas the Upper Lavas were erupted away from the axes. Feeder dykes (for lavas) are prominent in the Lower Pillow Lavas. A characteristic and easily recognisable feature of the succession, as the names suggest, is pillow structure, formed by tongues of lava swelling to a pillow shape during subaqueous extrusion. Individual pillows, some of which can be quite large, usually have a very fine grained or glassy rind due to rapid cooling. Small gas cavities, rarely exceeding 5mm in size, known as vesicles are present and are often lined with secondary minerals, such as calcite, chalcedony and zeolites. The vesicles indicate that the original magmas were rich in volatiles, though there is also an implication that the depths of the sea were not too excessive at the time. Hydrostatic pressure at great depths tends to prevent the rapid escape of dissolved gases from magma, so large and abundant vesicles do not develop.

The rock types in the lava succession are dominantly andesites, dacites, basalts and basaltic andesites, essentially a mixture of creamy white plagioclase feldspars, black-looking ferro-magnesian silicates such as pyroxenes, and iron ores. In the Upper Lavas green olivines are prominent, often in the form of large grains (phenocrysts), frequently replaced by calcite and iron oxides. In the Lower Lavas olivine phenocrysts are absent and any large grains that do occur are comparatively smaller and formed of plagioclase feldspars and pyroxenes.

Mineralisation in the ophiolite is largely confined to asbestos and chromite bodies within the ultrabasic rocks and massive metallic sulphide deposits in the lavas. None of these deposits are being worked currently on a large scale, most mines declining in the 1960's and eventually closing in the 1970's and 1980's (Itinerary 29).

The waste heaps of the huge asbestos mine on the eastern side of Mount Olympus at Pano Amiandos, now derelict, are an eye-sore, but were a very valuable economic asset. The asbestos occurs in veins, mainly as the hydrated magnesium silicate chrysotile, within a zone of intensively brecciated and serpentinised harzburgite.

Extraction of the sulphide deposits has occurred over many thousands of years, since at least 3000 B.C., but peaked in Roman times, between the two World Wars and in the immediate post-1945 period (Itineraries 8, 19, 25 and 26). Groups of disused mines and slag heaps in five mining districts scar the landscape around the flanks of the Troodos Range and Limassol Forest, none more so than at Skouriotissa. Although copper is only a minor constituent of the ores in which iron pyrites is dominant, it is the reason for the fame and name of Cyprus. The Romans called the metal *Aes Cyprium* (ore of Cyprus). The ores occur in relatively small lenticular bodies, a few tens of metres thick, and in stockworks (feeders) cutting through the lavas. They are prime examples of metallogenesis associated with rift-faulted zones along spreading axes, where plates are being pushed apart by the injection of igneous materials. The metals appear to have been precipitated in the stockworks, and on to the sea bottom, from hot, metal-bearing gaseous fluids. These fluids originated at depths of several kilometres in the hot ophiolite body, but consisted of reheated and recirculated sea water which penetrated along fissures at depth and leached out metals from the rocks. At the point of emission the 'normal' alkaline sea water reacted with the acid, hot gaseous fluid (c. 350 degrees C), probably creating 'black smokers', that is dense clouds of precipitated fine-grained metallic sulphides. These were laid down in the vicinity of the smokers, progressively building-up into stratiform lenticular bodies, shaped in detail by the form of the bottom topography. On consolidation, the ore deposits became immediately susceptible to submarine weathering, producing iron-rich multicoloured ochres, useful as colouring matter in paint pigments, stucco, mortar and cement.

Late-stage submarine hydrothermal emissions (hot springs), at temperatures of 10-20°C, also account for sedimented pockets of umber, a mix of iron and manganese oxides again highly prized by the Ancient Egyptians and the Masters of the Italian Renaissance as a pigmentation material (Itinerary 16). The umbers are part of the late Cretaceous (Campanian) Perapedhi Formation and on the northern side of the Troodos Range rest directly on the pillow lavas. This is in contrast to the southern side, where lenses of sedimentary breccia, up to 100m thick, rest unconformably on the lavas and commonly intervene between them and the umbers. The implication is of a more turbulent environment, sufficient to erode the upper levels of the ophiolite and redeposit the umber materials.

A prominent east-west fault belt, the Arakapas Fault Belt or Zone, separates the Troodos ophiolite mass from the Limassol Forest ophiolite mass (Itineraries 14 and 15). This fault belt extends along the full southern flank of the Troodos Range and probably eastwards beyond Larnaca. The range of igneous rock types exposed in Limassol Forest is similar to Troodos, but they appear to have had a much more complex structural history. There is strong evidence for solid deformation of the rocks both during and after their original emplacement. For example, repeated overthrusting occurred during Miocene times, and its consequences are seen especially well along the Yerasa Fault and Fold Belt (Itineraries 24 and 30).

The eastern and southern flanks of the Troodos Range and Limassol Forest comprise the fourth major physiographic zone of Cyprus. It is one of increasing geological complexity the further west, towards Paphos, one travels. It is also typified by impressive scarp and dip scenery, with major and minor escarpments of the gently dipping sedimentary succession facing inwards towards the mountains. The Middle Miocene Pakhna Formation escarpment in the vicinity of Pakhna is very impressive, though prone to landslipping, with altitudes reaching 700m along its considerable length. Although there are considerable thicknesses of older Cretaceous (Maastrichtian and Campanian) radiolarian mudrocks, bentonitic clays, sandstones with a high volcanic component and marls outcropping in this ground e.g. the Kannaviou Formation (about 80-65 million years old) northeast of Paphos (Itinerary 9), the bulk of the rocks creating the distinctive high relief scenery are Tertiary in age. They were uplifted and tilted in late Miocene times, about 10 million years ago, and again in Pleistocene times so that they are now excellently exposed, especially along the flanks of the numerous deeply incised river gorges radiating from the mountains. Chalks, chalky marls, limestones, conglomerates, calcareous sandstones and shales, clays and salt deposits characterise the Tertiary marine succession (Itineraries 2, 9, 10, 11, 18, 20, 22 and 28). Many of the deposits carry a sprinkling of feldspars and ferro-magnesian minerals, similar to those in the ophiolites, suggesting that the igneous masses were being subject to sea-bottom and, eventually, sub-aerial erosion during that long period of time (about 65 million years). Initially the deposits tend to be deep water (represented by the Lefkara Formation chalks, about 65-23 million years old) becoming more and more shallow water in type in passing through the Pakhna Formation (about 23-12 million years old) into the Koronia Member and Kalavasos Formation and eventually sea-margin Athalassa Formation rocks in Plio-Pleistocene times (about 5-3 million years ago). Most of the deposits carry significant numbers of foraminifera, free-floating multi-chambered micro-organisms, and these can be seen using a hand-lens, though only the large bodied varieties are obvious. Of these, *Discospirina* which is about 5mm across, is probably most easily detected, especially when concentrated into distinct bands. In the Pakhna Formation such bands can be traced over considerable distances and are useful for correlation purposes (Itinerary 10). Microfossils are also a useful tool in working out the age of rocks and correctly fixing the time boundaries within successions, such boundaries commonly not co-inciding with changes in lithology. There are many problems of this type, waiting to be satisfactorily resolved, in the Tertiary succession.

The pure white chalks, which form a distinctive part of the Lefkara Formation, are very well exposed in the coastal zone to the east of Limassol and are a very important basic resource for the island's cement industry (Itineraries 7 and 8). Something of the order of 850,000 tons of cement are produced annually at the Vassiliko plant, near Zyyi. Though they are worked rather intermittently at present and on a small scale, the gypsum deposits of the younger Kalavasos Formation are also of commercial value. They formed in several shallow water salt basins around the flanks of the emergent Troodos massif during very late Miocene (Messinian) times, about 5 million years ago (Itineraries 8, 9, 18 and 28). The Kalavasos Basin to the east of Limassol and the Polemi Basin to the northeast of Paphos are two such, and three others are located near to Larnaca, Morphou and Nicosia. Messinian times were a period of marked sea-level lowering over the whole of the Mediterranean region and, more locally, significant tectonic uplift of the Troodos and Limassol Forest masses. The culmination of this episode of uplift is well seen along the southwestern edge of Limassol Forest, where southwards overthrusting defines the Yerasa Fold and Thrust Belt (Figure 2).

Mantling the Tertiary beds inland there are wedges of Quaternary breccio-conglomerates, conglomerates and sands, commonly exposed on the flanks of valleys (Itinerary 30). Many of these are scree or talus deposits formed of locally derived materials and are probably the southern equivalents of the fanglomerates of the Mesaoria Plain, though on a much smaller scale. They indicate intense sub-aerial weathering and erosion of the Troodos Range after the Miocene earth movements.

In the Paphos district, to a much lesser extent along the southern flank of Limassol Forest at Moni, and in a small outcrop just to the east of Ayia Napa, erosion of the Tertiary beds has created 'windows' through which is revealed a most intriguing and complicated structural pattern in the underlying late Cretaceous (Maastrichtian) rocks (Itineraries 3, 5, 6 and 23). The name Mamonia Complex is applied to these highly deformed rocks, named after a small village to the east of Paphos. An examination of the outcrops, a prime location being Petra tou Romiou on the southern coastal road, shows that they consist of very extensive sheets and blocks of a range of rocks, including sandstones, limestones, cherts and basaltic lavas, which are set in a distorted and sheared bentonitic clay matrix, rich in smectite clay minerals. The age of the rock masses extends from the Triassic to at least early Cretaceous, so they are not in the place where they originally accumulated. In fact, they give every indication of representing the break-up of a Mesozoic continental margin, originally located to the northwest and north of Cyprus, during a phase of plate convergence. This view is substantiated by the disoriented disposition of the masses, some being turned up on end and others overturned. There is a strong suggestion that they were deposited by slumping and sliding, and as debris flows, into a mud-filled basin on the flanks of the ophiolite masses. The French term melange is often conferred on these deposits in which the matrix is younger in age than the enclosed masses.

The Mamonia melange is highly faulted (and folded), especially along its margin with the Troodos Massif, and the evidence indicates marked compression and strike-slip movements during and after its emplacement. Sheets of serpentinite are associated with some of the faults, and these igneous rocks have affinities with the altered harzburgites of Troodos. Hence, they have been interpreted as re-mobilised ophiolite materials intruded along the faults and sometimes emerging from the faults as submarine lava flows. Additionally, at places such as Ayia Varvara 6km to the north of Paphos Airport and the Baths of Aphrodite west of Polis, there are narrow tectonically emplaced slivers of metamorphic rocks (marbles and schists), representing altered sediments and basic igneous rocks. Their origin is controversial, but possibly relates to dynamothermal metamorphic changes immediately beneath the ophiolite masses during obduction processes. What all these features mean is that the Complex, to a large extent, is a tectonised melange formed in the contact zone between the African Plate and the 'Cyprus Microplate' mentioned earlier. The final complication in the story is that of the reworking of the tectonised melange during subsequent earth movements, such that the masses and matrix were partially displaced by further submarine sliding as debris flows. The Kathikas Melange, named after a village 22km north of Paphos, and Moni Melange near Limassol, exemplify these less internally disrupted sheets of rock (Itineraries 9 and 24). As they are less broken-up by earth stresses, and the materials in effect are all of local origin, the deposits are called sedimentary melanges.

The coastal margins of southern Cyprus in many places have a low-lying flat relief, measurable at a few metres or tens of metres above present sea-level. These are thin spreads of Pleistocene and Holocene marine terrace (raised beach) and river terrace deposits resting unconformably on solid rocks, and laid down over the last 1.65 million years (Itineraries 4, 7, 11 and 12). The inland edge of the lower and younger marine terraces is commonly backed by a degraded ancient sea-cliff line. Gravels, sands, silts, marls and very fine dust-like alluvium carry a range of components derived from the ophiolite masses and their sedimentary cover. Where ophiolite materials predominate, as at Governor's Beach east of Limassol, certain layers, and even the adjacent beach sands, have a distinct greenish-grey tinge. Many of the marine deposits carry a rich variety of shallow and warm water fossils, such as the bivalves *Arca* and *Pecten*, and colonies of the coral *Cladocora caespitosa*. At least four marine terraces can be recognised, but the best displayed and most easily inspected occur at a height of 8-11m and 25m above present sea-level. The lower terrace of this pair is 185-192 thousand years old (late Pleistocene) and is well exposed at Coral Bay, north of Paphos and at Ayios Yeoryios and Governor's Beach, a few kilometres to the east of Limassol. These terraces and older higher level ones are witnesses to higher sea-levels in the not so distant past. The causes of these changes include worldwide variations in the volume of water in seas and oceans during the Pleistocene Ice Ages and, in Cyprus, intermittent uplift (obduction) of the Troodos ophiolite due to continual underthrusting from the south of Mediterranean crust beneath the Anatolian (Cyprus) microplate.

When successfully irrigated, the various terrace deposits can be horticulturally and agriculturally highly productive. In the Ayia Napa, Larnaca and Morphou areas the deeply reddened soils are ideal for potatoes, artichokes and citrus fruits, many grown for export. The soils are produced by the Mediterranean-style weathering and erosion of terra rossa soils, originally formed on nearby limestones. A feature tending to diminish the quality of the soils and their sub-surface drainage is the presence of hardened layers, known locally as havara or kafkalla. These are hard carbonate-cemented levels within the soil profile and underlying weathered rocks , sometimes a metre or more in thickness, and formed by the evaporation of ground water. If the top soil cover is washed away you are left with the hard capping, other names for which are caliche and calcrete.

Some of the youngest deposits in southern Cyprus are salts (Itineraries 12 and 13). They are precipitated in a series of shallow water lakes created landwards of coastal sand and gravel barriers during the last few thousand years. The salt, derived from sea water percolating through the barriers, is precipitated in the hot, dry summer season, mainly as rock-salt (halite), but gypsum, sylvite (potassium chloride) and Epsom Salts (hydrous magnesium sulphate) have also been found. The best known salt lakes are at Larnaca adjacent to the airport, though commercial working has now ceased. In its heyday, production reached about 5,000 tons per year. Another large salt lake, but non-commercial, is at Akrotiri, on the southwestern outskirts of Limassol.

ITINERARIES

1. AKAKI RIVER SECTIONS

Location. Sheet 11, K717 Series, 1:50,000. 25km SW of Nicosia, along the B9 and E903 roads leading towards Palekhori.

Summary. The three localities described below allow you to see in some detail part of the pillow lava succession which comprises the uppermost level within the Troodos ophiolite (see p. 10 and Fig. 4). The pillow lava succession averages about 1km in thickness hereabouts and on this northern side of the Troodos Range characteristically dips gently northwards at 10-30°.

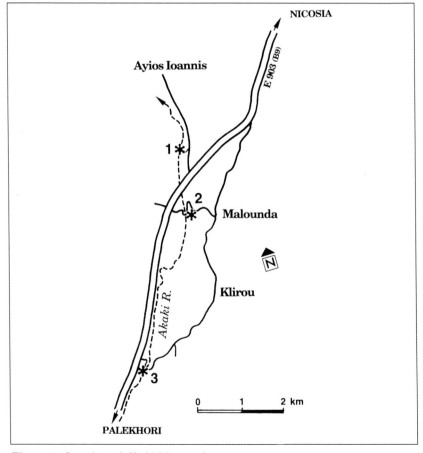

Figure 4: Locations of Akaki River sections.

The first stop (1) is adjacent to a minor crossroads at 166784, 1.2km due west of Aredhiou village and about 300m short of a large bridge across the Akaki river. Turn right northwards off the E903 towards Ayios Ioannis, signposted as 2km away, and after about 300m turn west opposite two small trees onto a dirt track which winds its way down to the riverside (166788). The track is suitable for fourwheel drive vehicles and very small coaches, though the walking distance from the metalled road is only about 250m. A prominent chalk escarpment, clearly visible between the olive trees, can act as a pointer to the route from the crossroads.

Near the bottom of the track and forming the face of the western bank are thinly bedded and mildly crumpled Middle Lefkara Formation chalks and marls of Upper Palaeocene age, dipping at about 30° to the northwest. The Lefkara Formation to the north of the Troodos Range is much thinner than its equivalent succession to the south and seems to have been laid down in relatively shallow waters. Certain of the thinner beds carry abundant trace fossils of the *Chondrites*-type; these are narrow oblique tubes of a sediment-churning organism. On the east bank, where you are standing, the chalks show a mild degree of faulting and four distinct minor faults downthrowing to the west can be seen cutting through the bluff. The relationship between the Lefkara Formation and the underlying Upper Pillow Lavas is essentially that of unconformity, with the chalks resting on the much older lavas, though the actual contact is not visible here. The faulting does not alter this relationship, though it might have affected the route of the river as it evolved during Quaternary times.

Now walk along the distinct footpath southwards, which is marked by a narrow water channel. Abutting the channel are a nearly continuous series of bluffs exposing, initially, excellent grey pillows of porphyritic olivine basalts and basaltic andesites within the Upper Pillow Lava succession. The general sense of dip within the lavas is about 10° due north. The traces of the original large olivine phenocrysts (which are now replaced by iron hydroxide-stained calcite) tend to be more obvious at the bottom of the pillows, where they accumulated under the pull of gravity whilst the lava was in a very fluid state. What is curious though is that olivines are also concentrated in the axial parts of some pillows, in what look like pipes, roughly circular in outline and as much as 30 centimetres across (Figure 5). This is particularly noticeable in pillows towards the base of the second bluff. It looks as though there was a late injection of olivine-rich lava through cylindrical gas cavities in the pillows, almost like toothpaste being squeezed out of a tube. The pillows vary in size and shape, the spheroidal ones being up to 75cm across whereas the ovoidal ones are up to 2.5m across. Note the very thin rind of what might have been originally glassy material around the pillows. This was caused by rapid chilling of the pillows against the sea water. Now there is a greenish tinge to the rinds denoting alteration into green smectite clay minerals. The pillows are also shot-through in places with irregular fractures and cavities; many of these tend to be occupied by secondary minerals including zeolites, such as clear to milky white analcite looking a bit like quartz, and fibrous radiating white to yellowish white natrolite. The presence of these zeolites indicates that the lavas have undergone a low degree of metamorphism soon after their eruption, probably due to reaction between the lavas and invasive heated-up sea water.

Figure 5: *Darker and coarser grained olivine-rich core in pillow of Upper Pillow Lavas. Scale in centimetres.*

Continuing further along the footpath brings you to alternating exposures of brecciated lava and pillow lava, faulted in places. The former are largely extrusive breccias, strongly iron-shot and calcite veined, caused by the physical disintegration of rapidly cooling lava as it flowed out of small volcano-like orifices or fissures along the irregular sea bottom. The precise location of these orifices is difficult to judge here, though they were probably well-spaced out. What one looks for are vents and feeder dykes cutting through the lava pile, but throughout the Upper Pillow Lava succession on the island such structures are comparatively rare. A good example of extrusive breccia occurs about 200m along the path in a 10m high steep bluff above the river (Figure 6). This bluff consists to a large degree of relatively small angular to sub-rounded fragmented pillows set discretely in an ashy matrix. The entire breccia is strongly veined by secondary calcite. Breccias are exposed for the next 80m then there is a return to 'normal' pillow lavas over the last 25m, where the path terminates.

Return to the main E903 Palekhori road and continue southwards for 1km to the next crossroads. Turn left down the slope towards Malounda (Malounta)

Figure 6: *Pillow breccia with broken fragments of pillows shot through with carbonate veins.*

and park against the old bridge across the river at 163775. About 20m from the eastern end of the bridge, and just off the metalled road, is a distinctive canyon-like side-valley down which a small stream, the Kamara Potamos, flows (2). A narrow pathway can just be discerned leading along the southern side of the valley through scattered trees. On the opposite side of the stream there comes into view, after a few tens of metres, an impressive south-facing wall exposing in some detail the nature of this part of the Upper Pillow Lava succession. The basalt and basaltic andesite lavas are darker and less vesicular than at the last locality. What are most impressive in the face, and you need to look closely, are large lobate structures which look like very large pillows, though the margins are rather irregular in detail with lobate offshoots. These 'megapillows' are between 2-10m wide and up to 4m thick. Radial cooling joints resembling rosettes are visible within the bodies and these are probably most easily picked out in the orange-brown weathered 'megapillow' located about 2m above the centre of the grassy slope. The bodies are interpreted as major feeder tubes acting as conduits for fluid lava passing through the lava pile. Just below the pillows you will find black glassy material which formed by explosive reaction between the hot lava and the sea water. The term hyaloclastite is used to describe the glass, because its constituents are in the form of small angular fragments or shards created during the very rapid cooling and disintegration of the lava. Chemical investigations of this material, which encapsulates most accurately the original composition of the lavas, shows that there are significant differences from the typical lavas that are poured out at spreading mid-oceanic ridges in modern oceans.

If you now cast your eyes to the lower part of the exposure you will be able to pick out tabular bodies of lava, a metre or so in thickness, which are not obviously pillowed. These are sheet flows typical of the lava succession throughout the ophiolite outcrop. Both here, and at intervals as you continue upstream, you will notice a distinct green tinge to the rocks which is caused by the presence of a secondary green clay mineral, known as celadonite. The presence of this mineral has been taken by some authorities as characteristic of the Lower Pillow Lavas. If so, it is likely that the boundary with the Upper Pillow Lavas occurs towards the bottom of the face, possibly at the base of the pillowed sequence and just above the hyaloclastites.

The stream bends southwards for about 100m and then, before you, there is a waterfall and plunge pool. The scramble up the right hand side of the waterfall is easy and some 5m above stream level you are presented with a splendid north wall to inspect (Figure 7). This is best seen from the bank opposite the face, as you can then try to work out the complexities of this part of the Upper Pillow Lava succession. The face consists mainly of sheet flows which have been affected by faulting. The most obvious fault is on the left-hand side of the face, the fault plane being etched out by weathering and erosion. The very prominent, rather massive-looking, columnar-jointed sheet flow is clearly affected by the fault and appears to be relatively downthrown on the left side. However, an alternative explanation is that the fault was already present, in the form of a small fault escarpment, on the sea floor before the sheet flow was emplaced. This could account for the thickening of the sheet flow to the left as it draped itself over the scarp feature. Cutting through the sheet flow is a very obvious thin dyke, which can be followed obliquely up the face, across the fault without any significant displacement then flattens to become concordant with the right hand sector of the flow. This is an example of a dyke passing into a sill. As you follow the line of this

Figure 7: *Faulted sheet flows (SF), dyke (D) and sill (S), Kamara Potamos. The thick sheet flow in the centre, faulted at the right-hand end, shows columnar jointing.*

intrusion through, note that it cuts a thicker dyke rising from the stream bed with a small waterfall, again without any deflection. This second dyke occupies a minor fault zone, and again the faulting occurred prior to the dyke emplacement. In summary, the sequence of events seems to have been (a) minor faulting of older sheet flows, (b) emplacement of a major sheet flow draping over the two faults, (c) intrusion of the thick eastern dyke, and (4) intrusion of the thin dyke-sill. The dykes acted as conduits or feeders for the sheet and pillow lava flows.

Return to the main E903 road and turn southwards for 3.5km until you see a T-junction leading off to the left and downwards towards Klirou. Park against the bridge across the Akaki river (3). Work your way down obliquely to the river for about 100m, keeping to the west bank and upstream side of the bridge. A rough pathway down can normally be made out and a very mild degree of scrambling is required.

What you now come upon is a spectacular cross-section through the Lower Pillow Lavas cut by a series of dyke swarms (Figure 8). There are three main rock units that can be recognised (a) hyaloclastites, (b) sheet flows and pillow lavas, and (c) feeder dykes. The dark grey to black hyaloclastites are well exposed at the foot of the cliff in a small embayment on the far side of the reddened strong ribs of the multiple dyke swarm which dominates the section. The pillow lavas are about 10m thick and beautifully exposed towards the top of the cliff. The pillows are more like bolsters in places and anything up to 5m long. Note the tonguing-down of some of the pillows into the underlying surfaces, a

*Figure 8:   Dyke swarms cutting through sheet flows, hyaloclastites (H) and pillow
          lavas (P).*

good way of telling that the lavas have not been overturned by subsequent earth-movements. Both they and the underlying, more scruffy-looking sheet flows carry chalcedonic silica and the zeolite heulandite, often in vesicular cavities. In contrast to the Upper Pillow Lavas the rocks tend to be non-porphyritic, that is they do not contain many large grains (phenocrysts), and overall they are lighter in colour, some having a pale green tinge. They appear to have been subject to a greater degree of metamorphism than the Upper Pillow Lavas.

The altered doleritic dykes, commonly showing very fine-grained, dark brown to black chilled margins up to 6cm wide caused by rapid cooling against the cold consolidated lavas, post-date the lavas here and almost certainly fed lava upwards to higher levels in the lava succession during the last stages in its history. The dykes are vesiculated and the vesicles (gas cavities), up to 3cm long, are elongated and aligned parallel to the margins. Chalcedonic silica occupies many of the vesicles. Also note the strongly developed cooling joints perpendicular to the edges of the dykes. It is an interesting exercise to work out the sequence of dyke intrusions using the same criteria outlined for the last stop. Five sets (or minor swarms) have been recognised based on cross-cutting relationships and angle of dip. Most of the dykes strike roughly north-south, but the angle of dip varies between 70-80° to the west and east. The older dykes are distinctly reddened due to oxidation of their ferromagnesian minerals, whereas the younger are a lighter brown. Go to it! The task could be simplified if you crossed the bridge and worked your way up to the high flat area facing the exposures. You need to walk up a dirt track behind the flat first, then scramble up a gentle overgrown path leading to the top. You then have a splendid overview, ideal for photography.

2. AMATHUS (AMATHOUS)

Location. Sheet 24, K717 Series, 1:50,000. 8km to the east of Limassol along the coastal road B1 (Figure 9). Grid reference 127412.

Summary. The sedimentary rocks at this site exhibit a range of storm-induced scour, slump and graded bed structures, together with compaction phenomena, within what is probably the upper part of the Pakhna Formation.

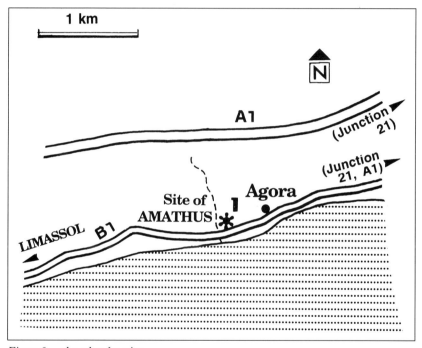

Figure 9:   Amathus location.

The location (1) is adjacent to the main western entrance to the archaeological site which, together with the rock-cut temple and the Agora site to the east, is worth visiting, though looters in the early 19th Century and later have destroyed a great deal. Amathus is probably one of the oldest city-states in Cyprus - eleven were in existence in the 5th Century B.C. – and is reputed to have been founded by a son of Hercules or by Amathusa, the mother of Cinyras. A Temple of Hercules flourished in Roman times, with a shrine to Aphrodite and Adonis. Under Roman rule Cyprus was divided into four administrative districts with Amathus being the local administrative centre of an extensive area covering parts of Troodos. St John the Almoner, founder saint of the Knights

Hospitaller, is said to have been born here in A.D. 609 and returned here to die. Richard Coeur de Lion, on his third crusade, landed near here in A.D. 1191 after bad weather had forced his fleet off-course. He deposed the tyrannical Governor and self-styled Emperor of Cyprus, Isaac Comnenos, married Princess Berengaria of Navarre in Limassol Castle, and was persuaded into the acquisition of Cyprus. He quickly disposed of it firstly to the Knights Templar and a year later to Guy de Lusignan. At that time Amathus was probably falling into decay, no doubt partly due to the effects of devastating earthquakes, land subsidence and changes in sea-level. Extensive, originally low-lying parts of the city now lie under the sea. Submerged foundations of old sea walls and buildings occur at depths of up to 15m, well offshore from the ruins of the old tower. A well laid out footpath, just above the main road, leads from the location eastwards to the Agora (market place) excavations. These have some fine marble and Pakhna Formation columns.

The geological exposures at Amathus, adjacent to the Temple Piano Restaurant, are readily accessible and occur in a recently cleaned-up cliff face, some 10m high, immediately to the west of the entrance path to the archaeological site. Parking is easy.

The rocks are well-bedded medium to coarse grained limestones which dip southeastwards at about 10°, carrying lenses of breccio-conglomerate. The age of these rocks is one of the problems with which geologists have continually wrestled. They appear to be concordant with the underlying Middle Miocene Pakhna Formation limestones and marls, exposed a short distance further up the gorge-like valley. In which case they are likely to be part of the Pakhna. There is much

Figure 10: The darker coloured load casts penetrating into the lighter coloured sediment beneath. Note the oblique flame structures at the base of the load casts.

Amathus

Figure 11: Convolute lamination layer sandwiched between undisturbed beds.

evidence that the Pakhna rocks in this area were being subject to earth movements towards the end of Middle Miocene times, with uplift and significant erosion by sea-bottom currents. The shallowing of the water readily accounts for the features described below. The south-facing slope of the crags on the west side of the gorge carry a thin mantle of younger Koronia Formation beds, which map out regionally as resting unconformably on various older rocks including the Pakhna.

The sedimentation features to look out for are (a) graded units, with coarse and sharply erosional bases passing upwards into finer grained, often thinly bedded and rippled tops; (b) contorted or convoluted layers up to 40cm thick, especially towards the top of the exposure and in adjacent crags; and (c) shallow, scour channels occupied by an assortment of angular fragments of locally derived materials. Many of the fragments seem to have had a soft marl or chalk composition so they have now weathered-out. All these sedimentary features point towards intermittent, but very powerful, currents moving sediment along and down shallow water shelf slopes, probably during very stormy conditions. The channel fills, an excellent example of which occurs towards the top left hand side of the face about 2.5-3m from the top, can be regarded as a type of debris flow initiated under those conditions, and the same is probably true for the graded beds. The fining-upwards grading indicates a progressive waning of the carrying capacity of the storm-induced bottom currents. The most intriguing structures can be seen about 2.5m from the top of the face and look like dark 'pillows', measuring up to 80cm in length and 40cm in height (Figure 10). These are load-casts, formed by the weight of quickly deposited and commonly coarse sediment pushing down into softer, finer sediment beneath. The displacement took place very soon after deposition of the coarse layer and led to the detachment of certain parts of it. The left hand cast is virtually isolated from its neighbours. At the base of the casts are oblique inverted V-shaped 'intrusions', referred to as flame-structures.

The origin of the contorted or convoluted thin layers (Figure 11) is probably by mild slumping of the originally soft sediment down the sea bottom slopes. An excellent example of such occurs 1m below the top of the face at the southern end.

Walking a few tens of metres northwards along the dirt track opposite the restaurant enables a glance across to the quarries on the other side of the gorge. There you can pick out about 1.5m of loosely consolidated coarse conglomeratic material resting unconformably on the solid rocks beneath. The pebbles are of mixed origin, some being derived from the local sedimentary succession, others from more distant ophiolite sources. They are essentially scree and downwash deposits of Quaternary age.

3. AYIA (AGIA) VARVARA (PAPHOS)

Location. Sheet 17, K717 Series, 1:50,000. 9km southeast of Paphos. Turn off northwards from the B6 main road near to Akhelia. A metalled road (E606) leads all the way to the outskirts of Ayia Varvara village 2km away (552456), where a left fork takes you in to the centre, followed by another left fork downslope. At the far northern edge of the village the road changes into a dirt track, which is very rutted in places, and winds roughly parallel with the Ezousas river on the left. Follow this track towards the rising ground, 1.2km distant (Figure 12).

Summary. This short itinerary illustrates the nature of the amphibolites and quartz mica schists, serpentinite bodies, basaltic olistoliths, marbles and basalts in the late Cretaceous tectonised Mamonia Complex.

Note: The Mamonia Complex rocks and structures at this locality are probably best appreciated if the simpler story at Petra tou Romiou and the Dhiarizos River section is examined first (see p. 97 and p. 41). Also refer to The Baths of Aphrodite itinerary (p. 35).

The ground immediately to the north of the village consists of intermittently exposed displaced masses of Triassic-Cretaceous rocks, some of sedimentary origin, known as the Dhiarizos Group (see p. 8). They form part of the tectonised melange within the Complex. This melange formed as a consequence of deformation brought about by a northwestern and western continental African Plate impinging against the 'Cyprus Microplate'. The masses can be seen on both sides of the river cropping-out as isolated crags in the fields, giving rise to a topography which is characteristic of major melanges in many parts of the world.

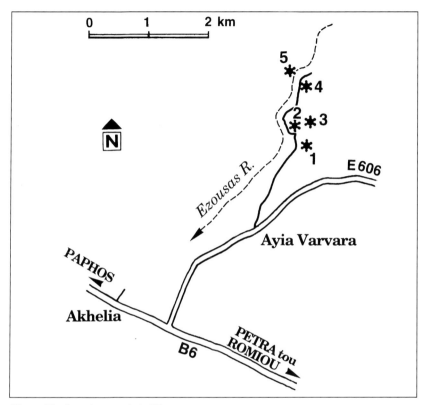

Figure 12: Locations at Ayia Varvara.

Typical examples of the Triassic masses are best inspected along the Dhiarizos river section (see itinerary 6, p. 41).

Just before you reach the dark-looking prominent craggy ridge, with an access path leading into disused road-metal workings, there is visible on the right-hand side of the track, and about 100m from it, a distinctive gleaming white disused quarry (559469). The main face is about 8m high. Use the east-heading footpath leading towards the south side of the partly overgrown quarry and cut across the cropped ground carefully at some appropriate point (1). The rock is a highly recrystallised limestone of Triassic age, looking like a marble. It does have a strong reaction with dilute hydrochloric acid, a simple test for calcium carbonates. When viewed under the microscope it has a breccia-like appearance, because the original rock is shot through with coarse calcite veins and patches. Small pockets of chert also occur. The original limestone was dense and fine grained, and there are vague outlines of foraminifera. It is probable that this was once a reef limestone laid down in relatively shallow seas. There are several similar bodies outcropping further up-slope towards the east and to the west across the river. Although the contact between this marble and the immediately surrounding rocks is hidden, detailed mapping of the ground indicates that the latter are likely to be submarine basaltic lavas, breccias and tuffs, set in a clay matrix. It is possible that the marbles were generated from limestone blocks incorporated into the hot lavas in Triassic times. The marbles and lavas were then displaced as a unit and incorporated into the melange. Polished, finely grooved surfaces, known as slickensides, and indicative of internal physical displacement, face some of the marble blocks.

Now head for the rough, pebble-strewn track leading up a moderately steep slope and into a road cutting giving access to the old workings (2). The crags and cutting expose the basaltic rocks just mentioned. At the bottom of the track the first crag on the left comprises non-pillowed lavas with polished slickensided surfaces, but in the cutting itself pillows are prominent. Many are red-weathered and carry phenocrysts of olivine of which some are now altered into iron oxides and carbonates. In the Mamonia Complex they are referred to as the Fasoula Formation (Dhiarizos Group) and are massive blocks probably of Triassic age, now incorporated within the melange. Their close relationship with Triassic limestones (marbles) becomes evident if you slowly work your way up the cutting. A large pod of marble occurs after about 50m, clearly caught up in the lavas and tuffs. On the east, right-hand side the pod abuts a near-vertical zone, 4m wide, of wavy-bedded, partly silicified basaltic tuff. This fine grained tuff gives every indication of having being sheared by fault movements. In fact, the whole cutting, which includes further marble patches, shows evidence of disturbance and faulting along east-west lines.

Beyond the cutting is the steep northeastern face of the original workings and this exposes metamorphic rocks belonging to the Ayia Varvara Formation (3). The full outcrop is triangular-shaped and measures about 1.6km from east to west and about 870m from north to south at its widest. The junction with the lavas to the south is a fault, running NNW-SSE here.

At the foot of the face are finely laminated metamorphic rocks, referred to as quartz-mica schists and amphibolites, the latter being darker coloured (Figure 13). The lamination is known technically as schistosity and is caused by the parallel orientation of minerals, especially platy-habit minerals such as silvery-white muscovite mica. When the schistosity is as pronounced as it is here then it is easy to measure its strike or orientation (083°) and its dip (54° north). Note that some of the planes of schistosity exhibit minor 'kink folds'. This indicates the schists were plastic at some stage in their genesis and capable of being refolded. The mineralogy of the quartz-mica schists is as the name suggests, but garnets and alkali feldspars are also present in some layers. There is a remarkable geochemical resemblance between them and the olistoliths occurring within the Dhiarizos Group. The schists are, therefore, metasediments. In contrast, the

Ayia Varvara (Paphos)

Figure 13: Schists showing characteristic lamination (schistosity).

amphibolites, which form the bulk of the Formation, are altered Dhiarizos basic rocks, or metavolcanics, and consist mainly of a mixture of dark calcic hornblende and plagioclase feldspar. Creamy green epidote is ubiquitous in the amphibolites, occurring as veins, pods and laminae up to 1cm thick. It is an alteration product of pre-existing lime-bearing minerals, such as occur in many igneous and sedimentary rocks. If you are fit enough and prepared to scramble up from the eastern end of the face to the slopes above and scout about, you will find plenty of chert lenses and schistose metaquartzites showing ample evidence of shearing, and white marbles. These are all further types of metasediments.

The origin of these metamorphic rocks is a subject for much debate. They are essentially the products of low grade 'amphibolite facies' metamorphism, and the mineralogy indicates that they formed at temperatures between 500°-700°C and at pressures between 3-10 Kilobars. Studies of ophiolite complexes in other parts of the World, such as in Newfoundland, have shown that beneath such complexes there is commonly a zone of metamorphosed rocks, which can be as much as 500m in thickness. Amphibolites and other varieties of schist are generated in this 'metamorphic sole', probably as the ophiolites begin to be physically displaced (obducted) during convergent plate movements. Many authorities believe that the heating necessary for this style of metamorphism is derived from the residual heat within the ophiolite plus a certain amount created by frictional forces during displacement. But there is an element of doubt about all these ideas.

There are several questions to be asked at Ayia Varvara. Were the metamorphic rocks generated beneath the Troodos ophiolite? If so, how did they become detached and tectonically upthrusted into the Mamonia Complex some 20km or so away from the present outcrop of the ophiolite? Or were they generated more locally from a hidden part of the ophiolite mass, assumed from geophysical evidence to exist at depth beneath the Mamonia Complex?

Return to the entrance track to the quarry and follow the main track leading off northwards. The track curves around on the flood plain, initially hugging the bottom of the lava crags.

A further 750m (4) along brings us to another important aspect of the Mamonia Complex story, because on the immediate left hand side of the track, where it deviates in a sharp curve down towards the river bed, there is a smooth surfaced, almost flat, rock outcrop, just below the level of the track, of highly sheared amphibolite (558478). The surface is only gently tilted and a careful look shows that it carries parallel grooves (slickensides). This probably indicates a low angle thrust fault, the general sense of movement which created the grooving being roughly northeast-southwest. Mapping of the Mamonia Complex has demonstrated that low angle thrust faults, trending approximately east-southeast – west-northwest, are commonplace and appear to bound many of the igneous and metamorphic rock units. In effect, this means that the Complex consists of an array of thrust-slices (and folds), leading to repetition at outcrop of some of the rock types. The thrusting post-dates the deposition of the Mamonia melange and is probably related to the compression of the melange as it came into juxtaposition with the more rigid Troodos ophiolite mass. This probably occurred when displacement of the ophiolite was taking place from late Cretaceous times onwards. The whole complex was subject to great stress in Miocene times especially, probably induced by strike-slip fault movements along the contact between the ophiolite and the melange.

Do not continue along the main track but follow a sidetrack on the left, about 60m away from the fault, down to the river bed. You are heading for the narrow track on the other side, which runs obliquely upwards to the northwest (5). The river is normally fordable at this point, but is easy enough to wade through on foot. The far side of the track exposes a rather complicated section through igneous rocks. At the foot of the incline are olivine basalt pillow lavas which carry gas cavities infilled with secondary calcite (amygdales). They abut sharply on their northern side a distinctive green rock, serpentinite, and the contact is probably a high-angle fault, distinct from the low angle thrust fault across the river. The fault plane dips to the south at about 45°. Serpentinites are rocks created by the hydrothermal alteration and mobilisation of ultrabasic and basic igneous rocks, such as harzburgite (see p. 11). A close inspection, using a hand lens, might just enable you to see the outline of the original pyroxene grains replaced by a fibrous green variety of serpentine called bastite. Ascend the track further and you are back onto basaltic pillow lavas.

The origins of the serpentinites in the Mamonia Complex are a bone of much contention. The original harzburgite, from which many of them appear to have formed, occurs in the deeper levels of the Troodos ophiolite outcropping to the north. So, it is possible that some alteration and mobilisation of harzburgites now hidden beneath the Mamonia Complex, took place during plate convergence, such that sheets of serpentinite were emplaced either along the line of thrust faults or by thrust fault movements.

There is an interesting angle on the serpentinites, well illustrated here at the upper contact with the overlying basalts. There you will see a dark chocolate-brown, fine grained zone, about 15cm thick, at the base of the lavas indicating chilling against the serpentinite. This means that the serpentinite might have been exposed on the sea-floor as a consequence of 'leaking out' via fault-controlled fissures; it might have been laid down as a lava flow, probably under high hydrostatic pressures because of the deep water environment. As we surmise that the serpentinites were emplaced in late Cretaceous times it then follows that the lava at this locality, with its chilled contact, must also be late Cretaceous in age and not Triassic. Again it appears likely that these particular lavas 'leaked-out' via some nearby active fault zone at the time. You can now perceive that the name Complex is totally appropriate.

4. AYIOS (AGIOS) YEORYIOS ALAMANOS

Location. Sheet 24, K717 Series, 1:50,000. 18km east of Limassol, exit 18 from the A1 motorway.

The entrance road is metalled as far as the convent of St George Alamanos, a somewhat quiet and forbidding building occupied by nuns. From then on a rough dirt track leads along a pleasant valley down to the pebbly beach (1) (Figure 14). There is abundant parking space.

Summary. This location gives an excellent opportunity to examine fossiliferous 8-11m late Pleistocene Raised Beach (or Marine Terrace) deposits, resting unconformably on Lefkara Formation chalks.

This is a prime location to see one of the major Raised Beaches, or Marine Terraces as some people prefer to call them, in Cyprus. Around the coastline of the island at least four such have been recognised and correlated with some degree of certainty. Correlation is not an easy business because exposures are not continuous and certain parts of the island might have tilted more than others since the deposits were formed. The oldest and highest at about 350m above sea-level is likely to be Pliocene and the next in age, at 100m and 60m, are Pleistocene. The one at this locality is also of Pleistocene age, but its altitude is much lower, generally at 8-11m above sea-level. The contained fauna has been dated as late Pleistocene by using radiocarbon methods and these dates indicate formation between 185,000 and 192,000 years ago.

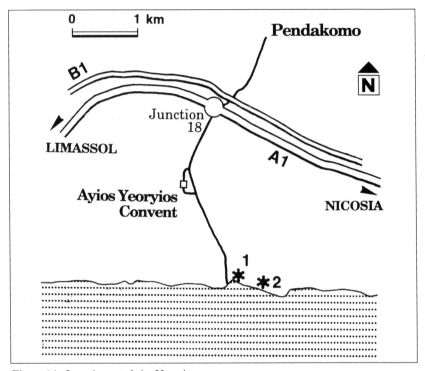

Figure 14: Locations at Ayios Yeoryios.

From the pebbly beach walk up to the cliff top. You can either go eastwards or westwards for about 2km or more in each direction along dirt tracks. The raised beach deposits are well exposed on ledges and in re-entrants all the way along and access is generally easy. Care needs to be taken on certain ledges poised above very deep water as loose material derived from the deposits can make footholds insecure. The base of the raised beach is very irregular in some places, and can be as little as 5m above present high water mark (2). In others, it is relatively even and flat-lying at a height of about 8m above high water mark. One of the controlling features is the differential erosion of the alternating harder and softer bands within the underlying thinly bedded, cream and white Lefkara Formation chalks. The discordance between the chalks and the overlying near-horizontal beach deposits is emphasised by the south and southwesterly dips in the chalks. On the western traverse these dips can be as high as 45° and the discordance shows up extremely well: whereas on the eastern traverse they are as low as 5° and the discordance is less obvious. Sea caves are prominent features at the foot of the cliffs in some places, where the sea has exploited major joint planes.

The raised beach deposits comprise lenticular seams and thin layers of coarse to fine gravels (or shingle) with sands and silts. Thicknesses reach at least 4.5m. They are variably cemented by calcite, which accounts in part for some layers being more prominent than others. At the top the degree of cementation is high as a consequence of calcretisation processes (see p. 17). If you look carefully at the basal gravels you will find pockets of fossils, commonly in a very well-preserved state. This seems surprising considering the origin of the deposits until you realise that the fossil fragments were probably washed down into the interstices between the pebbles, giving them some protection against excessive wear and tear by the waves. There are pockets rich in bivalves such as *Glycimeris*, 4cm across, *Cerastoderma*, *Parvicardium* and *Ostrea*. Others rich in gastropods, such as *Gibbula*, *Conus* and the limpet-form *Patella*.

5. BATHS OF APHRODITE (LOUDRA TIS AFRODITIS)

Location. Sheet 8, K717 Series, 1:50,000. 9km northwest of Polis (Poli) along a tarmaced road ending in a large car park with a Cyprus Tourism Organisation pavilion and restaurant (Figure 15). Grid reference 404798.

Summary. This itinerary mainly illustrates the amphibolites, quartz mica and calcareous schists, and serpentinites within the late Cretaceous Mamonia Complex. It also shows the Loudra tis Aphroditis basaltic pillow breccias and manganese-rich shales, and Akamas Sandstone olistoliths in the tectonised melange of the Mamonia Complex.

The site is one around which much romantic legend revolves. The Goddess of Love, Aphrodite, is reputed to have met her lover Adonis for the first time here when he paused to quench his thirst after hunting in the nearby Akamas Forest. Fable or not, this is a place of considerable charm and there is much of interest apart from the geology. There are well laid out and labelled Nature Trails leading from the pavilion via the famous pool and grotto (1) (located where the watertable is perched at a relatively high altitude above the nearby sea within permeable Pakhna Formation limestones resting on impermeable serpentinite) and the CTO, in collaboration with the Forestry Department, issue freely from their offices a well-illustrated pamphlet covering the characteristic plant life.

The Baths are situated on the northern flank of the Akamas peninsula with excellent views across Chrysochou Bay to the elevated western flank of the main Troodos ophiolite mass. The peninsula also has a foundation formed of ophiolite and, in effect, is a series of inliers structurally isolated by rift faults from Troodos and surrounded by a veneer of younger and unconformable Tertiary and Quaternary sediments. This fairly simple disposition of the rocks is, however, complicated by the presence of a zone of highly disturbed rocks, which outcrop intermittently wherever erosion has stripped away the veneer. These disturbed

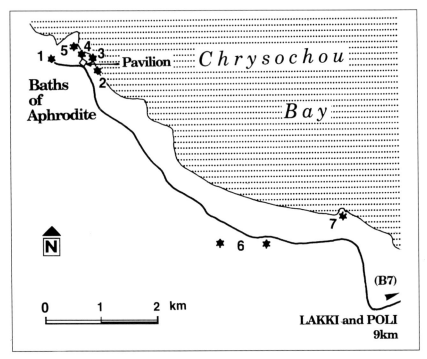

Figure 15: Baths of Aphrodite locations.

rocks now exposed along the shore at the Baths, and outcropping for about 2km to the northwest and 3km to southeast, belong to the late Cretaceous Mamonia Complex, an assemblage or melange of Upper Triassic to early Cretaceous materials laid down by gravity sliding and slumping, and subsequently highly faulted. For further details see p. 28 and p. 41.

Descend to the bouldery beach on the eastern side of the pavilion by a moderately wide winding track and walk eastwards for about 80m to look at what is known as the Loudra tis Afroditis Formation, a unified package of displaced rocks of Triassic age within the melange (2) (Figure 16). The first prominent outcrop consists of about 7m of chocolate brown, thinly bedded manganese-rich siliceous sediments representing very quiet phases of deposition during submarine volcanic activity. The manganese originated from the associated lavas. These are followed, after a 10m gap and adjacent to an impassable headland, by a mass of lava breccias up to 20m thick, with angular and rounded fragments of vesicular basalt and trachyte up to 40cm in size which are all set in a soft, sometimes cherty, matrix. Pillow structure is still visible in some of the fragments. In places you will be able to detect crude bedding which

Figure 16: Loudra tis Afroditis lava breccias (B) forming headland and manganese-rich shales (M) in bluff to right of figure.

implies that the breccias, derived from the break-up of lavas, were subject to redistribution by bottom currents in Triassic times. Typical lavas of this age are also seen at Petra tou Romiou, where they are generally unbrecciated and exhibit excellent pillow structure (see p. 101).

Now walk westwards along the beach. Just to the west of the track is a cliff exposing light creamy coloured schistose metacherts with some lenses, seams and pods of marbles up to 15cm thick (3). Note that the foliation, a secondarily induced structure caused by metamorphism, is nearly vertical and is striking roughly north-south. Continue along the bouldery beach past some overgrown concrete steps, which lead up to the pavilion, and past a rough steep path leading up to the cliff top and eventually you come to some dark-looking, angular-weathered rocks (4) (the rocky island opposite appears to consist of the same materials). Initially these are grey to black amphibole-rich schists (technically known as amphibolites and probably metamorphosed basic igneous rocks) with a fine lamination or foliation which dips at angles varying between 65° and near vertical. The trend of the foliation is now roughly northeast-southwest. It is very worthwhile examining these outcrops at the foot of the cliff in some detail for the next 200m or so. Pick a calm day as there is a moderate degree of scrambling required just above high water mark. As you traverse westwards note that the amphibolites are intercalated with quartz-mica schists in which some of the faces shine brightly because of the concentration of white mica (muscovite). Quartz veins up to 20cm thick are present. Note how the foliation planes are often refolded indicating that the deformation of the original sandy or silty sediments was carried out in several separate phases (Figure 17). As you progress around the small headlands you will find signs of intense brecciation and faulting of the schists with some brecciated and sheared zones and lenses up to 10m wide. Within the zones occur angular fragments of schist plus fragments of dark unfoliated ultrabasic igneous rock up to 25cm in size.

The origin of the metamorphic rocks is a puzzle and it is unclear whether they were emplaced within the melange by sliding at the same time as the adjacent Triassic blocks of lava breccia or whether they were structurally emplaced by thrust faulting at a later stage in the evolution of the Complex during the physical displacement (obduction) of the Troodos ophiolite mass (see p. 31). On the whole, the latter explanation seems more likely. Just beyond the schists in the first major embayment in the cliff-line appears evidence favouring structural displacement (5). A major high angle fault zone is well exposed separating brecciated schists from serpentinite, a hydrothermally altered and mobilised ultrabasic rock (probably a harzburgite originally) shot through with calcite veins (Figure 18).

The Mamonia Complex is characterised throughout its wide outcrop by serpentinites and this particular major sheet-like body at the Baths eventually swings southwards and continues for about 10km towards Paphos. The serpentinites create interpretative problems, especially as they are commonly bounded by thrust faults, as here. The widely held view is that they originated at a very late stage in the history of the Complex and mostly represent intruded re-mobilised, igneous magma emanating from subjacent ophiolite sources (see p. 16 and 106). In certain places the serpentinite bodies enclose displaced 'rafts' of schist, implying that their emplacement occurred later than the emplacement of the schists (see p. 43).

Now return to the pavilion and travel back along the main road towards Lakki (Lachi) for about 2.3km. The outcrop of the Mamonia Complex widens at this point and extends inland for about 2km. About 35m south of the roadside at 420782 and partly obscured by carob trees is a 4m upstanding mass of orange-red sandstone (6). Access is easy. The dip and strike of the sandstone is difficult to determine as it is highly jointed and disturbed by internal faulting; slickensides (finely grooved polished surfaces) are present. By looking west-southwestwards

Figure 17: Deformation by refolding in schists. Scale in centimetres.

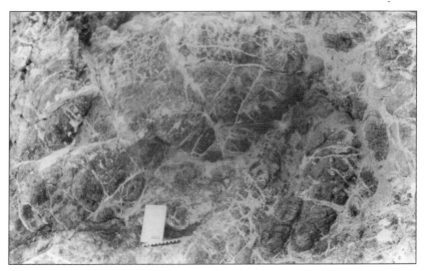

Figure 18: Serpentinite showing characteristic network of irregular veins. Notebook is 20cm long.

for about 500m across the fields, and more remote (150m) from the road, you will notice an even larger and much more prominent monolithic mass, about 15m high, of the same sandstone (416783) (Figure 19). These masses or blocks are again displaced from their original site of accumulation, just like the lava breccias at the Baths. They are known as the Akamas Sandstone Member of the Episkopi Formation, a group of rocks which vary in age from early Jurassic to at least early Cretaceous as opposed to the Triassic age of the breccias. The sandstones are very quartz-rich and have a simple mineralogy, indicating a maturity which could have been reached by prolonged reworking in a shallow water shelf (continental margin) environment. This does not necessarily mean a simple history, because studies have shown that prior to their lithification in Jurassic-Cretaceous times it is probable that the mature loose sediment was moved rapidly into a deeper water situation, possibly by sheet-flow mechanisms.

A very pleasant place to stop, finally, on this excursion is about 0.4 km further towards Lakki, where there are parking areas on the northside of the road situated on the Lower Miocene Terra Limestone Member (7). Although the upper surface of the gently dipping limestones is strongly calcretised it is still possible to find fossilised colonial corals. For the botanically minded, however, the real treat at this locality are the abundant wild orchids.

Figure 19: Akamas Sandstone olistolith.

6. DHIARIZOS RIVER SECTION

Location. Sheets 17 and 22, K717 Series, 1:50,000, 18km southeast of Paphos. Turn northwards off the main B6 coastal road onto a metalled road leading towards the eastern side of the rather obvious Asprokremmos (Asprokremnos) Dam. This lead-off road is on the eastern side of the road bridge. About 2.5km further on, and past the dam, the road forks to the right for Nikoklia and the very attractive deeply entrenched Dhiarizos valley (Figure 20).

Summary. These exposures of olistoliths comprising Vlambouros Sandstone, radiolarian cherts, deep-sea limestones and basaltic breccia and lava together with serpentinite bodies and metamorphic schists are within the tectonised melange part of the late Cretaceous Mamonia Complex and are best examined in conjunction with the exposures at Petra tou Romiou (see p. 97). Also see Baths of Aphrodite, p. 35.

The dam (1) across the Xeros River valley was completed in 1981 and services the agricultural and horticultural activities along the adjacent fertile, relatively flat coastal area as far as Paphos. It is built on 50m of permeable Quaternary marine terrace and river terrace gravels, sands and silts, some of these occupying a buried channel beneath the eastern abutment. The bedrock is faulted Pakhna and Lefkara Formation limestones, sandstones and marls of relatively low permeability, but well jointed and bedded, dipping at about 10° to the south. In view of the technical difficulties of the site, allied to Paphos being in an area affected by earth tremors, the dam has a self-sealing rolled clay core plus a well-compacted and graded gravel 'shell'. The bedrocks are grouted to a depth of 45m and a 3m wide 'cut-off trench' infilled with bentonitic clay and rolled clay acts as a curtain preventing significant seepage through the overlying Quaternary deposits. Water feeds into the reservoir from adjacent rivers and is also pumped in from several wells put down into nearby river gravel aquifers.

After the dam site, the first rock exposures to be visited are located about 2km beyond the outskirts of Nikoklia, at a sharp left hand bend in the road around a rocky crag (632438) (2). Directly opposite on the valley side you can see the virtually abandoned village of Souskio.

This exposure exhibits a good cross-section through a large displaced mass of sedimentary rock displaced in late Cretaceous times by slumping and sliding on the sea bottom. The succession exposed within the crag, which extends for about 80m along the road, is known as the Vlambouros Formation and is part of the Ayios Photios Group of the Complex. It is dominated by alternations of red calcareous sandstones, siltstones, bioturbated mudstones and limestones dipping initially at about 25° to the south. At the northern end the beds are acutely folded and fractured. The massive, well-jointed sandstones stand out from the weathered face and are worthy of close inspection, because on the upper surfaces there are a number of small linear bulges. These are sole structures, which might appear to be a bit of a misnomer until you appreciate that all these beds have

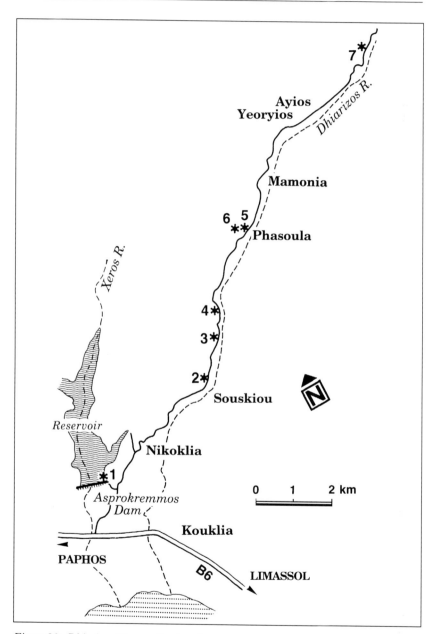

Figure 20: Dhiarizos River valley locations.

been inverted. Sole structures are commonly created by powerful sediment-laden currents in the sea, which scour the soft bottom sediment and create a range of small scale depressions, such as grooves. If you examine some of the finer grained sediments you will find black, carbonised plant debris. In some of the limey beds calcareous algae, sea-urchin, coral and foraminiferal debris of late Triassic age have been found, together with ooliths, which originate in shallow warm waters. However, detailed investigation suggests that the original loose sediment was swept off marine shelves and deposited quickly in deeper waters during Triassic times. The movement and inversion of the whole lithified mass occurred subsequently, of course.

The next stop is 1.25km further on, where brecciated basaltic lavas, probably of the Triassic Loudra tis Afroditis Formation (Dhiarizos Group), are well exposed on the western side of the road (640448). The locality (3) is well marked by an independent limestone block on the river side of the road. The break-up of the lava was by a process known as auto-brecciation in which the cooled surface disintegrated under the pressures exerted by the still moving hot interior. Blocks of lava with slickensided surfaces, caused by the physical displacement of the mass in Cretaceous times, are present and there is a certain amount of secondary white mica distributed throughout, indicative of a mild degree of metamorphism at some stage in their history.

From these basalts it is worthwhile walking along the road for the next 600m to inspect a whole galaxy of outcrops of masses of red and pale green, thin sandstones and interbedded marls of the Vlampouros Formation. The bedding in the exposures shows a range of dips, many vertical or near vertical, with apparent overturning.

At the end of the traverse, again on a sharp left hand bend in the road, there is a splendid exposure in an olistolith formed of dark brown to light brown, thinly bedded Dhiarizos Group radiolarian cherts and mudstones (643454) (4) (Figure 21). The beds dip at about 20° to the northeast. There is a small fold at the top of the face. If you glance across the valley you will see similar chert beds showing vertical bedding. The cherts are very hard, brittle and have razor-sharp edges, so be careful in handling the material and definitely **do not hammer** the face. Radiolaria are free-floating, single-celled marine micro-organisms with a siliceous skeleton and their circular outlines can sometimes be picked out with a hand lens. These deposits are generally thought to have accumulated originally, in Jurassic times, in relatively deep seas.

2.3km further on at the northern edge of Fasoula (Phasoula) village is a prominent south-facing craggy feature formed of another displaced mass, this time of Triassic olivine basalt lavas (5). These pillowed Fasoula Lavas outcrop near to the roadside. If you work your way on foot westwards for about 500m along the strike of the moderately steep slope, making a detour through the village, you eventually come across exposures, just beyond the last buildings, in what is a major sheet-like serpentinite body (6). The serpentinites in the vicinity

Figure 21: Radiolarian chert olistolith with thin bedding and lamination picked-out by colour variations.

of Fasoula are intrusive, probably emplaced along thrust faults, post-dating the emplacement of the melange (see p. 33). If you look at the low cliff at the eastern (village) end of the exposure you will find enclosed rafts (xenoliths) of amphibolite up to 3m in length, which were probably incorporated within the serpentinite from some deeper ophiolite-related source beneath the complex. Amphibolites are a variety of schist and here are rich in black amphiboles, albite, chlorite and epidote. If you now clamber up above the small cliff for a few metres you will also pick up several xenoliths of vesicular basalt, one measuring 7m by 75cm. These were possibly derived from the nearby Fasoula Lavas during the intrusion of the serpentinite.

The final stopping place along this traverse (708496) is not the easiest to locate (7). The route is via Mamonia and Ayios Yeoryios, and is 3km beyond the outskirts of the latter village, where the road side falls away steeply to the braided river bed. There are well terraced slopes opposite and on one, to the east-northeast, is a prominent small white church. Regrettably, the roadside exposures are not too impressive, consisting of scree of fragmented, shaley-looking laminated limestones. Nonetheless, these fine grained limestones are interesting in containing megafossils, especially bivalves. One thin shelled variety is *Halobia*, which lived in relatively deep seas. Rare ammonites and radiolaria have also been found, indicating a late Triassic age. This particular mass of limestone is small, but there are many much larger displaced masses distributed throughout the Mamonia tectonised melange. They are collectively known as the Marona Formation and are part of the Ayios Photios Group.

7. GOVERNOR'S BEACH

Location. Sheet 24, K717 Series, 1:50,000. 23km east of Limassol. Exit 17 on the A1 motorway (Figure 22). Grid reference 250415.

Summary. This location exhibits gently folded and faulted Lefkara Formation chalks and cherts, which are capped by fossiliferous late Pleistocene +8m Raised Beach deposits.

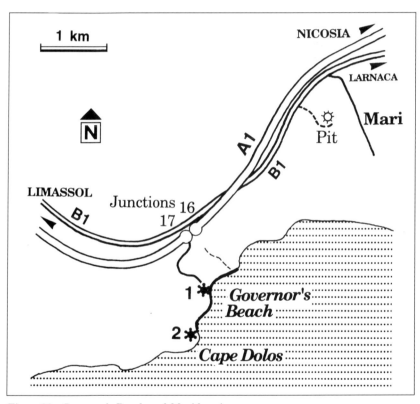

Figure 22: Governor's Beach and Mari locations.

The well-labelled access road from the motorway to the popular beach is tarmac for a few hundred metres, but soon deteriorates into a number of well-defined and well-used potholed dirt tracks. As there is much new building in progress between the motorway and the sea, the likelihood is that the transit across to the beach will improve. The best route in 1993 involved turning right at the first T-junction, where you are facing a new housing complex, then after a 100m or so bear left (southwards) off the tarmac road. You are heading for the

Panayiotis Cafe, a popular venue which is located on the cliff top adjacent to a small but prominent headland and above a narrow, dark green tinged beach (1). Access to the beach is via steps at the cafe, where there is abundant parking space. To the east, and somewhat marring the view, is the Zyyi cement works and to the south, though more visible from the cliff-top just to the west of the cafe, is the low-lying Cape Dolos.

Descend the cliff at the cafe and proceed along the cliff foot if sea conditions permit. The width of the beach varies somewhat and may be impassable at some points during high tide and stormy conditions. When this rare situation arises access to the beach still remains easy via several gullies a short distance to the northeast of the cafe.

The unusual colour of the beach is due to a relatively high proportion of epidote, black and green ferromagnesian mineral grains and dark coloured basic igneous pebbles. These materials have been recycled. They have been eroded from some source rocks, transported, laid down and then re-eroded several times over a long period of time, extending back through at least the Quaternary. In the first place, the materials were derived from the ophiolite masses, now exposed well inland, which consist of igneous rocks, such as basaltic lavas and gabbros rich in pyroxenes, olivines and chlorites.

The main reason for visiting this locality, however, is to look at the sedimentary rocks forming the low cliffs. At the base are the chalks of the Lefkara Formation which are of Palaeocene to Oligocene age here, and on top is a capping of less well consolidated and much younger Pleistocene raised beach (marine terrace) deposits.

The Palaeocene Middle Lefkara seen below the cafe is a creamy chalk, rather massively bedded but cut through by many vertical joints and several small faults. The beds are dipping at about 15° to the west, though it will become apparent towards the end of the 500m traverse that the dip directions have changed to about 15° east, clear evidence of gentle folding, probably during late Miocene times. The chalks are open sea pelagic deposits and carry a very rich microfauna, mainly of foraminifera which, unfortunately, cannot be seen clearly with the naked eye. They were laid down as organic oozes on the sea-bottom, but have now lithified. Just to the south of the steps there is evidence of channelling within the chalks, indicating that the sea-bottom currents were sometimes very active. Probably the most striking thing about the beds is the presence of very distinct brown, hard but brittle, chert seams and nodular layers (Figure 23). These usually parallel the bedding planes. At least a dozen seams are visible varying in thickness from a few millimetres to about 20cm. Chert is a siliceous rock which commonly forms secondarily in soft chalky oozes by the dissolution of siliceous organisms, such as Radiolaria and sponges, followed by re-precipitation of the silica when an adequate concentration has been reached in the pore water. The process starts early in the oozes, but it commonly takes

Figure 23: Secondary chert layers in Lefkara Formation chalks. The Upper Lefkara chalks in the distance are reddened and are surmounted by the Pleistocene raised beach.

several million years before the chert acquires the character as seen now. The fact that there are many seams separated by non-silicified chalk levels indicates that there must have been pauses in the deposition of the chalk allowing the silica to concentrate sufficiently for precipitation. If you look carefully you will notice that a few chert seams and nodules cut across the bedding. In at least one instance the chert runs along a fault plane, in some instances along other fracture surfaces. These must be second generation cherts formed some time after the bedded cherts and post-dating the minor faulting.

Another feature of the chalks adjacent to the steps, and a few tens of metres further northwards, is a very distinctive close-spaced fracture cleavage, the planes of cleavage being generally near vertical, but varying in trend. Cleavage of this kind develops in already hardened rocks due to concentrated earth stresses during fold and fault movements. It was almost certainly created at the same time as the gentle folding and minor faulting of the rocks, in late Miocene times.

A series of embayments and reefs as you progress in an easterly direction exposes massive brilliantly white, chert-free chalks of the Eocene Middle Lefkara. There are several exit points via steps to the top of the cliffs. These chalks are succeeded, at the end of the traverse and just to the east of a major re-entrant and dry valley bed, by thinly bedded chalks and marls of Upper Lefkara Formation (Oligocene) age, dipping to the east. Some layers are strongly bioturbated, others show variations in colour being distinctly pink or red, a feature of the Upper Lefkara in this area. The colour is caused by iron oxides and hydroxides produced from the breakdown by oxidation of pre-existing iron-bearing minerals in the chalks, such as iron pyrites and ferro-magnesian minerals of igneous origin, probably derived from the ophiolite masses. It seems likely that the breakdown occurred at the surface of the chalky muds during pauses in deposition. The sea would have been becoming shallower at the time.

Figure 24: Late Pleistocene raised beach deposits (R) resting unconformably on the Lefkara Formation (L).

All the way along the beach traverse, keep casting your eyes up to the top of the cliff, and note the presence of the 8-11m Raised Beach (or marine terrace), comprising gravels, sands and silts, which has an age calculated as being between 185,000 and 192,000 years, that is late Pleistocene. It is beautifully exposed in cross-section, especially immediately above the reddened Upper Lefkara beds, and is accessible in many places along the traverse (Figure 24). Large boulders of a wide variety of rocks (chalks, limestones and basic igneous rocks) characterise the base of the raised beach, which rests with very marked discordance on the Lefkara. Large whole valves of bivalves, such as *Pecten* and *Glycimeris* poke out from between the boulders and these are very useful for radiocarbon dating of the deposits. The Tusk Shell *Dentalium* is very common. At the very top of the cliff are weird and wonderful pebbly overhangs which are the uppermost levels within the raised beach. They have been subaerially, secondarily cemented by calcite (calcretisation) over several thousand years to become relatively resistant to weathering and erosion.

If you want to examine the calcreted surfaces more closely then it pays to walk about 500m in the opposite direction from the cliff-top cafe towards Cape Dolos (2). It takes about 15 minutes, or even longer if you dally in several other beach cafes adjacent to a pleasant wide sandy beach en route. The objective is easily picked out as a series of caves at the foot of a 2-3m high cliff. The capping for the caves, which are carved in the softer Lefkara chalks, is the hard calcrete. Boulders of coarse gabbro originating from the ophiolites are strongly cemented into the calcrete in places. But what is more intriguing are patches of green beach sand which have been washed up by storms onto the surface of the calcrete and now are cemented to that surface. Clearly a certain degree of cementation by calcium carbonate is still taking place and this is confirmed if you inspect further cemented gravelly and sandy patches at the foot of the cliff. The product of this modern cementation is referred to as beach rock. In hot climates it is brought about by precipitation from carbonate-rich sea water which has splashed over and into the loose beach sediment. In this respect it differs from the processes bringing about the formation of calcrete (also known as havara or kafkalla on the island) (see p. 17).

8. KALAVASOS

Location. Sheet 20, K717 Series, 1:50,000. 30km east of Limassol, turn north onto the E106 from the A1 motorway at junction 15 (Figure 25).

Summary. This itinerary demonstrates the Kalavasos Formation salt deposits (highly contorted in places), the reddened Upper Lefkara marls and Middle Lefkara Formation chalks, and the ore mineralisation in the pillow lavas of the Limassol Forest ophiolite.

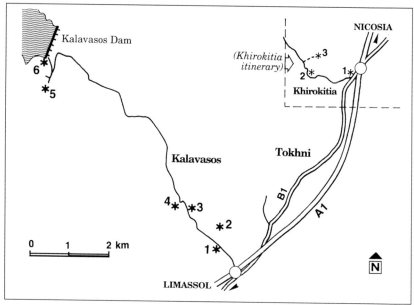

Figure 25: Kalavasos and Khirokitia locations.

Park at the roadside 1km from the A1 junction, just beyond a prominent white bungalow located 50m up the slope from the road, and you will see on the eastern side of the road a number of dirt tracks leading off to the east and northeast (1). You can walk along or drive carefully along any of these, but the most convenient curves gently uphill to the northeast and then turns sharply to the east. What you are heading for is a whole series of old gypsum quarries within the Miocene Kalavasos Formation, about 500m away (2) (282471). The workings are obvious and extensive, though the degraded faces and spoil heaps are somewhat overgrown, so it is difficult to measure accurately the thickness of the beds. There appears to be about 14m of the succession exposed, dipping at 10-15° to the south. A few decades ago gypsum was being extracted and exported in some quantity.

Gypsum deposits of equivalent age also outcrop to the south of Tokhni and near Maroni, a few kilometres away, so it is probable that there existed in this area in Miocene times a marked depression, probably a reef-bound lagoon extending east-west at the margins of the sea, suitable for gypsum precipitation (see p. 124 and 85). The seas occupying the Mediterranean region as a whole were undergoing marked evaporation and desiccation at that time, about 6 million years ago, not only because of climatic factors but also due to other physical changes, which isolated them from the open oceans to the west and southeast (Tethys). Movement of the Arabian Plate against the Eurasian Plate seems to have been the main culprit bringing about this isolation.

The best thing to do in these workings is to work your way around slowly from the most northerly faces to those on the eastern and southeastern sides, looking at the different forms the gypsum takes. The most spectacular is that of large blades and rosettes of transparent selenite. These are secondary re-crystallisation products of the original gypsum which, in contrast, commonly occurs with a sugary texture or in a very fine grained textured form as creamy alabaster. The beds vary from having a massive internal structure, with an even texture, to being laminated (marmara). The former indicates lengthy continuity in the chemical and physical conditions of deposition, whereas the latter implies rapid variations in those conditions.

In the most southeasterly quarry, marked by large and rather dangerous-looking 10m high face, is a 2m thick contorted gypsum layer. It is about 6m up from a flat ledge at the head of the quarry and is reached by an obvious path leading up to the ledge. This layer probably indicates slumping of pre-formed primary gypsum beds down shallow slopes at the bottom of the sea. It is identical in its characteristics and position in the succession with the one found near Tokhni, 1km to the east (see p. 124), and implies that the cause of the slumping was some regional event, such as a contemporary earth-tremor. This tremor probably being caused by further movement along some old deep-seated fault, located in the ophiolitic basement rocks.

Return to the road and head towards Kalavasos village. After about 750m there begin excellent exposures, on the right hand side of the road beyond the cemetery, of sediments constituting the Middle and Upper Lefkara Formation (Eocene-Oligocene) (275476). The section (3) is almost continuous down into the valley bottom for about 300-350m. The beds at the beginning of the section dip gently to the southeast at about 15°.

The Upper Lefkara is characterised by alternations of brown-buff coloured, thinly bedded limestones, and fissile marls and calcareous shales. They are very rich in foraminifera (microfossils), which can sometimes be picked out with a hand-lens. Bioturbation by a range of soft-bodied organisms is widespread and indicated by the traces of fine tubes running obliquely and horizontally through the sediments. Very thin films of breccia, carrying angular fragments of lighter coloured limestone, up to 7cm long, indicate a mild degree of scour by sea bottom currents.

A notable feature of the top of the Upper Lefkara is patchy reddening. At least two such reddened levels can be picked out here in the faces. The cause of the reddening is the oxidation of pre-existing iron-bearing minerals in the sediments, such as pyrites and ferro-magnesian minerals. This seems to have occurred on the sea-bottom during pauses in deposition, probably when the depth of water was diminishing due to relative sea-level changes.

Descend to the bottom of the slope, where you can see an old preserved mineral ore locomotive and wagons which were used for transporting ore from the copper mines, some 6km further up the valley, to Vasilikos on the coast. On the opposite side of the road inspect the chert-free brilliantly white chalks, which are a very characteristic lithology of the upper part of the Middle Lefkara Formation (Eocene) in southeastern Cyprus. The beds vary in thickness. They were laid down in comparatively deep waters by a slow, but persistent, accumulation of calcareous skeletons of Foraminifera and other micro-organisms. The beds are so strongly jointed that the amount of southeasterly dip is difficult to determine.

The old disused, large and rather scruffy quarries on the other side of the river (4) (272476) are accessible and comprise, in contrast, thinly bedded Middle Lefkara chalks of Palaeocene age, with sporadic chert nodules. The quarries are a good viewpoint to look at the geometry of the outcrops on both sides of the valley to decide whether there has been any displacement by a major fault, which has been inferred to be running roughly north-northwest – south-southeast along the line of the valley.

Continue through the village, along the very narrow main road which is unsuitable for coaches, northwards to the Kalavasos mining area. This comprises 13 ore-bodies, located at the boundary between the Lower and Upper Pillow Lavas of the Limassol Forest ophiolitic mass and known to have produced between them over 4.5 million tonnes of ore between 1937-1977. The bulk of this came from underground working, though in the 70's opencast working methods were preferred. The ore was predominantly pyritic with subordinate amounts of sphalerite (zinc sulphide) and copper pyrites (chalcopyrites). The copper percentage of the ore reached 2.5 per cent.

1.2km north of the village the tarmac road forks right, whereas the wide dirt track you need to follow forks left along a very pleasant valley heading towards Kalavasos Dam 4km further on. The Lefkara chalks soon give way to pillow lavas, which crop-out intermittently all the way to the dam.

The basalts and interbedded volcaniclastic sediments, including umbers, are severely disturbed by faulting and folding and, as a consequence, the succession dips steeply northwards at angles averaging 65°. The unconformable overlying sediments, in contrast, are almost horizontal. There appears to be a close relationship here between the east- and northeast-trending faults and the ore bodies; the fractures acting as natural conduits for the mineralising fluids from depth.

The ground on the left-hand (south) side of the track is now well vegetated with occasional spoil heaps and adits. They are disappointing for the collector of minerals. It is much better to carry on as far as the dam, because located some 300m south of the south end of the dam is a well exposed opencast pit, the Kalavasos Mine (5) (238503). This mine is readily visible and is marked by extensive spoil heaps, a shaft head winding gear, adits and, unfortunately, a smelly rubbish dump. If you can stand the smell, penetrate along the bottom of the pit looking at the mineralised lavas, but especially at the bright orange-yellow ochre, an iron-rich capping to the orebody caused by submarine weathering and oxidation. Downwashings of Lefkara chalks occur in places.

The dam itself, with metalled access road cutting through pillow lavas and lava breccias, is an excellent picnic spot (6). The southern abutment is characterised by a swarm of thin dykes cutting through the lavas and dipping at about 45° eastwards.

9. KANNAVIOU AND DISTRICT

Location. Sheet 17, K717 Series, 1:50,000. Kannaviou is about 26km northeast of Paphos, via the B7 Polis road to 1km south of Stroumbi, then turn off eastwards along the E703 Polemi – Kannaviou – Pano Panayia road (Figure 26).

Summary. This a circular scenic tour looking at the late Cretaceous Kathikas sedimentary melange, the volcaniclastic Kannaviou Formation, pillow lavas of the Troodos ophiolite, Miocene gypsum beds of the Polis Basin and sedimentary olistoliths within the tectonised late Cretaceous Mamonia Complex.

The village you are heading for initially is Agios Dhimitrianos and a road junction adjacent to sign indicating Paphos 24km (1). This is a splendid viewpoint overlooking the Ezousas Valley to the east with Kannaviou village nestling in the bottom. The first objective is the clearly landslipped area (2), looking like colliery waste heaps, on the slopes to the north, so turn left off the main road and after a short distance turn right onto a newly metalled road heading downwards and northwards towards Kritou Marottou village.

The material on display in the slip faces, which extend down to the roadside, at 593646 1km south of the village, constitute part of the Kathikas Melange (Kathikas Formation). It is a sedimentary melange, or olistostrome, formed by a number of deep water submarine flows of clay, silt and boulder debris, derived mainly from nearby unconsolidated Mamonia rocks during a late Cretaceous (Maastrichtian) phase of earth movement. This melange has a very wide distribution throughout the southwest region of Cyprus and attains thicknesses of up to 270m. It rests unconformably on Kannaviou Formation, Mamonia Complex and Troodos ophiolite sequences, all slightly older but also of late Cretaceous age, and is relatively undeformed and mildly faulted compared with them. The boulders and fine grained matrix in which they are set reflect the composition of the underlying source rocks and include fragments of

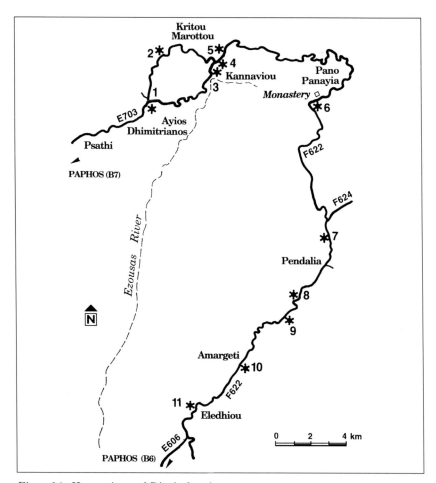

Figure 26: Kannaviou and District locations.

volcaniclastic and shallow water sandstones, shelf and deep water limestones, radiolarian cherts, pillow lavas and other basic igneous rocks. At this locality the boulders, which are up to 2m in size, are set in a reddish brown, weathering-grey, bentonitic silty clay matrix.

If you have the time and inclination to study this patch of slipped ground in greater detail you will find that the top of the melange is capped by bedded, gently dipping Lefkara Formation chalks. The passage is not as abrupt as the colour change indicates as conglomeratic lenses, patches and thin seams reworked from the melange occur at the base of the chalks.

Continue through the village then turn downhill into Kannaviou village (3). Turn right at the T-junction and stop on the northern outskirts in an obvious deep road cutting with a sweeping lefthand bend and village exit signpost (613643). Here are exposed light grey-brown, fine to medium grained volcaniclastic sandstones, which are part of the Kannaviou Formation. On the east side of the cutting the rocks are very strongly jointed and massively bedded, so the dip is difficult to determine. But on the west side more thinly bedded layers indicate a dip of about 30°, roughly southwards.

An interesting characteristic of the sandstones is their content of fragments and minerals derived from the erosion of the Troodos ophiolite and Mamonia Complex rocks. But, there is also a richness in pumice-like material, some fresh, of a both basic and acid igneous nature. Pumice is not known to be associated with the extrusion of ophiolite basaltic lavas, so that other sources must have been contributing to the sediment, probably located to the west, outside present-day Cyprus.

The Kannaviou Formation in this region reaches an estimated thickness of 750m and apart from volcaniclastic sandstones includes bentonitic clays, siltstones and basaltic conglomerates and breccias, the last resting directly on pillow lavas of the Troodos ophiolite. If you walk along the road northwards away from the village for about 50m you will be able to see in a small face the contact between Kannaviou sandstones and pillow lavas (4). It is marked by a narrow zone of brecciation which affects both types of rock. Is this a faulted contact? Or is the breccia erosional in origin having accumulated as a scree at the foot of a contemporary fault-controlled escarpment and then been overlaid conformably by the sandstones?

If you now continue beyond the T-junction and along a very pleasant valley, used by the locals for picnics, there are a series of good roadside exposures, as far as the bridge, of pillow lavas, brecciated lavas and sandstones (5). The outcrops are much affected by thrust faulting with fault planes dipping gently to the southwest. All these thrusts post-date the emplacement of the nearby late Cretaceous Mamonia Complex, though it is difficult to pin-point their exact time of origin.

The basaltic lavas are typically pink-brown in colour with pillows less than 1m in size and belong to the Upper Pillow Lava Series of the Troodos ophiolite. Initially they were rich in green olivine phenocrysts, but those have altered into a mixture of calcite and iron oxides. Gas cavities (vesicles) are often infilled with calcite, associated with the zeolite, analcite.

If you now want to round off this trip properly continue via Pano Panayia (the birthplace of President Makarios) to the monastery of Chrysorrogiatissa (Our Lady of the Golden Pomegranate), 3km to the south. The present buildings date from about 1770, although the settlement appears to be much older and established by the monk Ignatius in the 12th Century with 70 brethren. The monastery is noted for its icons and wines, recently introducing for sale its own special Monte Royia wine.

2km to the south of Panayia is the magnificent viewpoint and picnic site at Papa Loykas (6) (650631). The setting is beautiful and the panoramic views westwards across the Ezousas valley are splendid. The ground in front of you is much affected by landslipping, but on a clear day it is easy to pick out Kannaviou and a large mass of serpentinite outcropping on its southern flank. The brown weathering Kathikas Melange outcrops stand out well and the capping of Lefkara chalks.

Continue southwards along the F622 road via Statos until you reach the road junction with the F624 and a signpost indicating Paphos 36km (654587). This is another splendid viewpoint looking east, with the Troodos massif looming in the background to the northeast (7). The well-grassed and slightly hummocky ground sloping down in front shows gullied outcrops of the Kathikas Melange with slumped masses of Lefkara chalks. In the middle distance are larger scar-like faces of chalk.

Pendalia (Pentalia) is located on the late Cretaceous Mamonia Complex, the source of some of the materials in the Kathikas Melange, and for 1km both north and south of the village there are good outcrops at the roadside and in adjacent fields of some of the large blocks or olistoliths of Triassic sandstone within the Complex. About 2km south of the village and where the road has a double sharp bend, virtually opposite a rarely used church at Ayios Minas (8), is a good outcrop of serpentinite, a hydrothermally altered ultrabasic rock (642562). Serpentinites are a characteristic feature of the Complex and mostly are in the form of intrusive and thrust faulted sheet-like bodies. A further kilometre along (638556) are more examples of sandstone olistoliths with bedding dipping northeast at 15° (9). The sandstones are very hard, quartz-rich, coarse to medium grade and closely resemble the Akamas Sandstones (Jurassic-Cretaceous) found in the Mamonia Complex, west of Lakki (see p. 38).

At Amageti the new village bypass (623538) exposes rocks of a totally different type from those seen so far (10). The light brown marls interbedded with thin chalk seams outcropping here and dipping 10° to the southwest belong to the Kalavasos Formation (Miocene). The feature of interest, and particularly well seen on the east side of the road cutting, are several secondary concretionary masses, anything up to 5m x 4m in section, composed of very coarse radiating twinned blades of gypsum. These cut across the bedding in the sediments and are thus secondary in origin, probably growing as a consequence of salt-rich brines percolating through the soft bottom sediments.

The 'salt story' is carried further some 2km south of Amargeti, at the north end of Eledhiou village (11) (6055524). There, an obvious artificial cutting on a side track leading westwards from the gently curving main road exposes at least 8m of high quality gypsum beds. In the sides of the cutting are 4m of coarsely crystalline gypsum beds resting on 4m of finely banded gypsum (marmara), and these rest on gypsiferous marls near the entrance. What you are seeing here and at the Amageti exposure are expressions of salt deposition in a small basin (the Polemi Basin) during a marked phase of sea-level lowering and desiccation in the Mediterranean region during late Miocene times (see Tokhni and Kalavassos p. 119 & p. 49).

If you are returning to Paphos the route south of Eledhiou takes you on to the new E606 road. For 2km the route is over gently dipping Tertiary chalks and marls but then it drops down back onto the underlying Mamonia Complex rocks as far as Ayia Varvara and the Quaternary coastal belt. The road cuts through a wide array of easily accessible masses of rock (olistoliths) incorporated into the bentonitic clay matrix of the Complex and if you want to test your skills at identifying rocks now is your chance. The rocks to look for include thinly bedded creamy radiolarian cherts and red radiolarian mudstones, red marls, sometimes highly contorted and showing vertical bedding, marbles and pillow lavas. Remember that many of these blocks are of Triassic age and were incorporated into the late Cretaceous Complex by sliding and slumping. Serpentinite sheets also turn up at intervals.

10. KHIROKITIA (CHOIROKOITIA)

Location. Sheet 20, K717 Series, 1:50,000. Junction 14 on the A1 motorway, 32km from Limassol and Larnaca, 48km south of Nicosia (Figure 25).

Summary. This short itinerary demonstrates the nature of the *Discospirina* marker band in the Pakhna Formation and the spectacular channel fill deposits associated with the Pakhna Formation.

The road towards the village of Khirokitia takes you past the foot of the steeply rising and oldest known Neolithic settlement in Cyprus, which appears to have been abandoned round about 5250 B.C. (1). The site was discovered in 1934 and excavations have proceeded intermittently ever since, uncovering the characteristic circular foundations of what are now believed to have been flat-topped huts. Burials took place beneath the hut floors. The site is open all year round.

The first locality is about 1.4km beyond the Neolithic site and is at a very sharp and dangerous right-hand bend in the road, which here is skirting the southern side of the village (305507). Park your vehicle about 50m beyond the road-side church and about 50m short of the bend (2). On its inner core is exposed about 5m of chalks, marls, limestones, sandstones and siltstones belonging to the upper part of the Pakhna Formation (Middle Miocene). The base of the succession here consists of thinly bedded chalks which contain small smooth bivalves intermingled with a very distinctive flat and spirally ornamented benthonic foraminiferan, known as *Discospirina*. This has a diameter reaching 6mm, so is not difficult to see, once you have 'got your eye in'. Your best chance of finding it is in loose fragments, more especially at the point where the road does an abrupt turn. Attacking the rock face is unnecessary and usually unproductive. Because *Discospirina* is so distinctive it has proved very useful for correlating beds of equal age and in this area the band containing it has been traced for at least 27km along the strike of the beds from Kalavasos, just to the west, to near Kiti in the east. In about the middle of the face is a 40cm thick coarse limestone rich in bivalves and foraminifera which has very sharp contacts, expressive of very rapid deposition and scour by currents. Above that are thin marls, siltstones and limestones. The whole sequence gives every indication of having being deposited in shallow seas.

The road continues downwards along the foot of an escarpment for 250m until you reach a T-junction with a dirt road leading-off to the right (304510). Park at this point and walk along the dirt road to another T-junction with a partly metalled narrow road, leading up to the village. Turn right for about 50m then you will spot a slightly overgrown, but distinct, path off to the left which slopes down to valley bottom. Follow this to the dry bed of the Potamos tou Ayiou Mina (3). The cliff which you should now face is on the south bank of the river (Figure 27). The view is spectacular, for what you are looking at are two virtually superimposed channels cut into Middle Pakhna Formation rocks and filled with boulders and pebbles of very variable size and composition. It looks even more spectacular if you cross the river bed and move up the track to a higher viewing level. Then you will be able to see the lower major channel clearly and the upper one, about two-thirds of the way up the cliff, which is slightly off-set to the right. In the lowest and deepest-cut channel there is a boulder of Lefkara Formation chalk 2.5 metres across. Chalk materials are common, but there is also a good sprinkling of local Pakhna rocks as well as basic igneous rocks, such as altered basalts and microgabbros, with clear affinities with the Troodos and Limassol Forest ophiolites. All these rock types can be examined in the many fallen blocks at the foot of the cliff. But you need to exert some care, as certain blocks have fallen from the top of the well-bedded succession and these include coral-bearing limestones of the Koronia Formation, which caps the Pakhna hereabouts. It is clear from the channel fill materials that the older Eocene, Lower Miocene and Middle Miocene sedimentary rocks, and the late Cretaceous ophiolites, were being subject to intensive erosion at the time of formation of the channels. Notice that within the lowest channel there are dark brown, easily weathered seams of silt, only a few centimetres thick. These represent pauses in the successive stages of infilling, when the transporting currents were moving very slackly.

Figure 27: Tertiary channel deposits carrying boulders of Lefkara Formation chalk.
The base of the channel is indicated and curves upwards behind the author.

The geometry of these bodies strongly indicates that they are part of the
Pakhna succession and represent massive downslope movements of coarse debris
by powerful sea-bottom currents, possibly triggered-off by prolonged phase of
widespread earth movements or earthquakes. Deposits of similar type occur at
Tokhni, 3km away (see p. 121). They appear to be a variety of channelised
debris flow. Alternatively, the deposits could be much younger in age than the
geometry implies and could be Pliocene. If that is so, then the channels could
have been carved predominantly on a land surface as by that time large tracts of
Cyprus-to-be were emergent above the sea. What do you think?

11. KOUKLIA

Location. Sheet 22, K717 Series, 1:50,000. Roadside exposures adjacent to the
main B6 Paphos-Petra tou Romiou coastal road. 22km east of Paphos, 4.8km
west of Petra tou Romiou. Grid reference 618387. The Sanctuary of Aphrodite
and the site of the ancient city of Palea Paphos are nearby (Figure 28).

Summary. This location exhibits abnormally intensive folding in the Pakhna
Formation and the contact between the Pakhna and a late Pleistocene Raised
Beach.

These are comparatively small, but interesting exposures at a T-junction on
the north side of the busy main road, opposite a large notice board advertising
the 'Paphos Irrigation Project'. First, walk up the side road for 100m and on its
eastern side below a distinctive conical-roofed metal hut you will see, in a 5m
high face, an excellent cross-section through a small anticlinal flexure, faulted

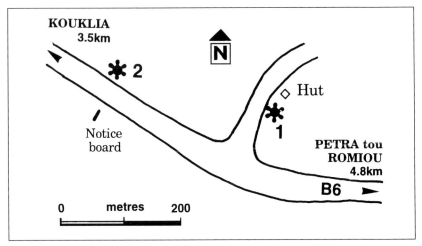

Figure 28: Kouklia locations.

along its axis which runs roughly east-west (1). The thin lenticular beds belong to the Middle Miocene Pakhna Formation and comprise alternating calcareous sandstones, limestones and marls. Certain of the harder layers show basal scour structures and contain fragmented angular pebbles derived from the underlying layers. Shell fragments are present (see p. 133). Now return to the main road and walk westwards towards a prominent roadside crag exhibiting the same rocks, but now strongly folded and steeply upturned so that they have vertical and near-vertical dips (2) (Figure 29). The axial plane of the fold appears to be curved, trending initially northwards but then swinging round to the east. There

Figure 29: Vertical Pakhna Formation sediments.

also is a certain amount of internal shearing or contemporary erosion within the beds, leading to the 'cutting-out' and truncating of some layers.

The structural disposition of these beds is curious, because as you have just seen the bulk of the outcrops hereabouts show gentle dips, mainly southerly and of the order of 5-25 degrees. A high degree of up-turning consequent on subsequent faulting, possibly in late Miocene times, might be the answer to this anomaly. It might even be that there is a major structure located in the ophiolite foundation at depth below the present outcrop, and that controlled the way in which the beds buckled.

Another interesting feature at this locality is the contact of bouldery raised beach (marine terrace) deposits with the solid Pakhna rocks. It can be seen just above road level at the western end of the exposure and is at approximately 25m above present sea-level. Deposits at a similar altitude at Yeroskipos, 18km to the west, have been dated as being at a minimum 43,900 years old, which means the beach deposits are late Pleistocene in age, older than some of the other raised beach deposits visited in this Guide (see p. 33 and p. 49). Cyprus is noted for its raised beaches. They are also reported at 50m and 100m around Paphos. Some authors have identified six on the west coast, ranging in elevation from 5m to 350m. All that we need to understand is that they indicate changes in relative sea-level, often due to the upheaval and differential warping of the Troodos mass and its sedimentary envelope during late Tertiary and Quaternary times.

12. KOURION DISTRICT

Location. Sheet 23, K717 Series, 1:50,000. Area immediately to the west of Limassol (Figure 30).

Summary. This itinerary illustrates the Miocene Pakhna Formation sedimentology, and that of various Pleistocene and Holocene deposits, including the western Akrotiri peninsula tombolo and the salt lake.

The Kourion (Curium) archaeological site, with its entrance now at the eastern end (899359), via the Curium Theatre Road East, is a must for visitors to the district and is open all year round (1). It has a complex history and 'many ages scatter their ruins over the bluff' (Thubron). There is evidence of occupation from Mycenaean times between the 14th and 12th Centuries B.C. onwards. It was populated by Greek immigrants from the Argos area of the Pelopennesus in 1595 B.C., one of whom might have been called Koureus. Pasicrates, the last King of Kourion, supported Alexander the Great in 332 B.C. in the naval siege of Tyre, supplying both ships and crews. Prosperity was retained under the Romans, and some of the remains of this period (30 B.C. – A.D. 330) are now the best preserved, despite the extensive destruction by an earthquake in A.D. 365. The theatre, only fairly recently excavated and rebuilt,

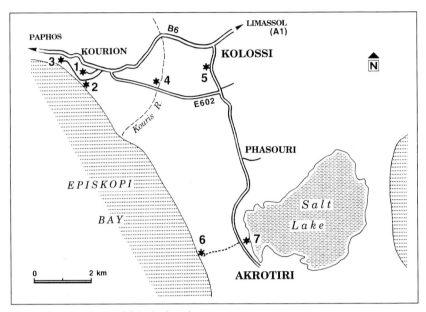

Figure 30: Kourion and District locations.

is sited with magnificent views over Episkopi Bay and across the fertile
Quaternary flatlands towards Akrotiri. In A.D. 45 and 47 the influence of visits
by Saints Paul, Barnabas and Mark to Cyprus saw a progressive conversion to
Christianity and that is reflected in the remains of the basilica at the western end
of the site. This is thought to have been the cathedral church of the Bishops of
Kourion in the fifth century. Local stone and an array of imported or re-cycled
marble bases and capitals, and granite pillars were used in its construction. The
site was not abandoned until the Arab raids of the seventh century.

The rocks forming the foundation of the site belong to the Pakhna Formation
(Miocene) and comprise a succession of calcareous sandstones, limestones and
marls dipping at about 5° to the south. They are best inspected at Kourion
Beach, at the foot of the site. But before you leave the historical site, and while
you are at the Roman theatre, cast your eyes southeastwards along the low-lying
coastline to the distant promontory of Cape Zevgari, 11km away. The cape is at
the western end of a ridge some 9.5km long and up to 60m high which forms the
southern extremity of the Akrotiri peninsula. It is formed of calcrete-capped,
shelly Plio-Pleistocene Nicosia and Athalassa Formation beds resting
unconformably on partly cross-bedded Pakhna Formation beds. The connecting
link from Kourion is a gravel and sand barrier, technically known as a tombolo
(an internationally known example is Chesil Beach in Dorset, England). It is

breached at one point only, where the Kouris river discharges intermittently into the bay. On the eastern, Akrotiri Bay side of the peninsula there is a similar feature connecting Limassol via Lady's Mile Beach to Cape Gata. The tombolos have a complicated and lengthy history, probably extending back into Pleistocene times. They are commonly initiated as spits attached to headlands during pauses in sea-level rise or during rises in sea-level, but from then on elongate and self-perpetuate by a process almost akin to cannibalism. At some point in time they clearly connected with the offshore islands at Akrotiri. Eventually, there came into being a protected low-lying area to their rear suitable for a quieter style of sedimentation. At present this is represented by a body known as the Akrotiri Salt Lake.

If you want to inspect the constituents of the tombolo at its northern end take the wide dirt track leading around the foot of the cliffs, towards an array of tavernas. Where the track first meets the gravel beach and turns through 90° is as good a place as any (2) (895356). The average size of the pebbles is about 20cm and if you look carefully you will be able to identify chert, limestone, calcareous sandstone, schist, serpentinite, pyroxenite (sometimes pegmatitic), gabbro, dolerite and basalt fragments.

Continue along the dirt track as far as the prominent cliffed headland. In doing so you travel across a relatively flat zone between the beach and the cliffs. This area was once inundated by the sea, probably during the Pleistocene and late Holocene, but since then has silted-up behind the tombolo. The base of the cliffs represents the position of the shore-line during those earlier times. Fine windblown sand is now piled-up in places against the cliff bottom.

The Pakhna Formation cropping out in the cliffs, especially the bottom 10m or so shows excellent lenticular bedding, large scale cross-bedding and channelling (3). One such scoured-out channel is about 80m across. All these features indicate quite powerful sea-bottom currents at the time of accumulation. If you look closely at some large inverted fallen blocks near to the beach you will see some lobate sole structures measuring up to 75cm x 50cm on some faces. These are also indicative of strong scour activity. Some of these blocks show a mild degree of bioturbation, with tubes or burrows up to 10cm x 1cm, implying that there were quieter phases of sedimentation interspersed with the stormier periods. Comminuted shell debris is widespread in most of the beds. Finally, note the fault in the cliff adjacent to the sea. There appears to be a displacement downwards of the honeycomb-weathered and cross-bedded strata to the south of about 30m.

Return to the main Limassol road (B6) and after 100m turn sharp right onto the E602 'Military road' along which you travel for 2km to the bridge over the river Kouris (922355). Park at the entrance to the dirt track leading northwestwards from the bridge (4). Follow the path leading off to the right and you are immediately confronted by a small, but striking, cliff, about 5m high, consisting of very fine grained, structureless and highly calcareous brown silt, carrying small carbonate concretions and a sprinkling of land snails shells. This material appears to be of alluvial origin, laid down by origin precursor of the present river during late Pleistocene times. Microscopic examination shows that it contains ferro-magnesian minerals of ophiolite origin and a few detrital micas.

The faces increase to about 10m height as you continue along this path and within them you will be able to see extensive bodies of coarse river gravel, rich in dark coloured ophiolitic material and local Pakhna Formation rocks. The gravels are very strongly cross-bedded in places and occupy scoured-out channels. They are interbedded with alluvial sands and silts. Towards the top of the exposures there has been a variable amount of secondary calcite cementation (calcretisation) which binds the loose material firmly into something resembling concrete. The gravels have been intermittently worked for road aggregate until quite recently, but the small scale of the operation has not proved to be commercially viable.

About 200m along the track note the incoming of fine grained orange-brown sands at the bottom of the cliffs, below the overlying alluvial deposits. It is difficult to judge whether these are part of the alluvial sequence or whether they are older deposits of an earlier age. If the latter, they are probably local representatives of the Nicosia Formation (Pliocene).

A short diversion to Kolossi Castle (940361) is worthwhile and it is open all the year round (5). The foundations date from A.D.1210 when it was built for King Hugh I of Cyprus. He gave it to the Knights Hospitaller, also known as the Knights of the Order of St John of Jerusalem, in 1302 but, after a troubled period, they departed to Rhodes leaving just a military presence behind, the Commanderie. This comprised some sixty villages, many involved in the production of wines reputed then to have had 'the flavour of goat and tar'. The castle suffered badly from Genoese and Marmeluke (from Egypt) attacks and was rebuilt around A.D. 1454. Further restoration by the British occurred in 1933.

If you want to continue your inspection of the tombolo travel southwards to about 2.5km south of the road junction at Phasouri and just to the south of a mass of radio aerials. Adjacent to a small white concrete hut is a 15m-wide dirt track leading off westwards. The track is negotiable for land-rover type vehicles all the way to the coastline. The target point is the easily visible rusting wreck of a small coaster (6). The walk from the main road takes about 30 minutes.

The track eventually takes you across the site of very extensive gravel workings, now infilled, which were once a prime source of aggregate in Cyprus. These gravels had the advantage of being reworked by coastal currents and waves, so removing softer materials. There is a much higher proportion of relatively hard ophiolite pebbles here than at Kourion. An interesting feature of the seaward face of the tombolo is a thin layer, up to 30cm thick, of beachrock. The layer extends into the distance on both sides of the shipwreck and is as much as 25m wide in places. It dips gently at 15° degrees towards the sea. Close inspection shows that it consists of secondarily calcite-cemented sand and pebbly layers, the cementation occurring in the wavesplash-zone. This process is widespread around the coastlines of hot climatic regions and is almost certainly continuing here at the present day. The precarious balance between precipitation of calcite from warm permeating sea water, with consequent stabilisation of loose beach sediment, and erosion due to storm conditions is evident with large broken slabs of beachrock having been thrown onto the top of the beach.

Return to the main road which is directly opposite what is now the western flank of the Akrotiri salt lake (7). The lake occupies the site of a gentle downfold in the Plio-Pleistocene Athalassa Formation and contains a significant, though shallow, cover of water only after a prolonged wet winter. The input of fresh water even then is very limited. It is tempting to believe that this was not always so and that several hundred years ago an arm of the Kouris river emptied into the northwestern corner of the lake depression. Ancient maps of 1573 (unknown hand) and 1630 (Mercador) appear to confirm that view. These maps also indicate that the lake site was then a permanent marine embayment with a persistent narrow channel opening-out to the east. At present there is no such constant connection. Thus it is intriguing that the peripheral salt marsh zone at present is characterised by the presence of abundant bleached valves of marine molluscs, such as solid shelled *Cerastoderma edule* and thin-shelled *Cerastoderma glaucum* and *Parvicardium exiguum*, together with gastropods. They clearly reflect a marine connection, though *C. glaucum* and *P. exiguum* can tolerate low salinities. In the dry season it is possible to walk across the desiccated mud surface of the lake, noting the glistening blades of precipitated salt, mainly gypsum. Some sea water might overwash into the lake during on-shore storms, more especially just to the northeast of the chapel of St Nicolas of the Cats (002293), but the bulk of the salts probably emanate via subsurface percolation of sea water through the tombolo sands and gravels.

13. LARNACA (LARNAKA) SALT LAKES

Location. Sheet 21, K717 Series, 1:50,000. Adjacent to Larnaca Airport on the lake side of the B4 road (Figure 31). Grid reference 575612.

Summary. This is one of the classic coastal salina locations where salts are being precipitated annually. Fossiliferous Pleistocene rocks may be observed. The mosque (tekke) of Hala Sultan, one of the holiest Islamic places, is nearby.

There are a series of lay-bys within a short walking distance of a prominent, but low, bluff facing the lake at the foot of which is a preserved section of the old road (1). A short distance to the right of the bluff there is the rather incongruous sight in winter and spring of football goalposts emerging from the surface of the lake.

You are standing on the southern edge of what is the main salt lake, which has a maximum depth of 3m, and is commonly frequented in winter and early

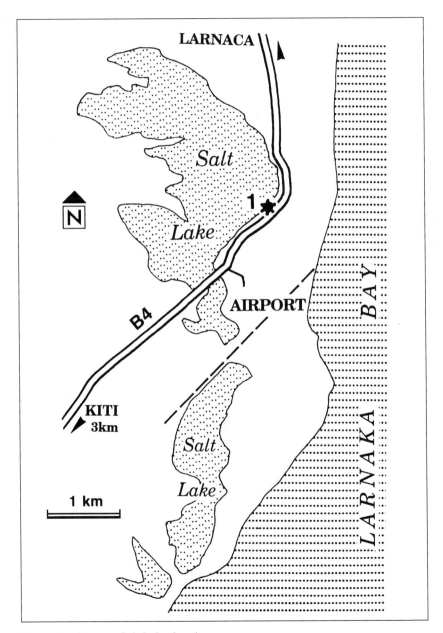

Figure 31: Larnaca Salt Lakes location.

spring by flamingoes. There are four such bodies at present, isolated from each other somewhat artificially by roadways and the airport runway. The most southerly is Dzezar Lake separated from the open Mediterranean sea by a sand and gravel barrier only some 200m wide. The lakes are classic examples of coastal salinas separated from the sea by barriers of varying width, attaining their present basic shape over the last few thousand years. They have been a subject of speculation since the time of the Natural Historian Pliny the Elder, a victim of the destruction of Pompeii in A.D. 79. The lake levels, even when the lake is full and relatively fresh after the winter rains are slightly below sea-level, so there is a natural hydraulic gradient established in the permeable gravels, sands and sandstones forming the barriers, sloping down from the open sea to the lake. Salt water percolates slowly through the barriers and into the lakes at all times of the year. In the hot dry summer period, when lake levels are lowering rapidly due to evaporation, salt water may percolate even more readily into the bottom waters and sediments of the lake. It is in the summer season that maximum precipitation of salt occurs as a type of surface encrustation, a few centimetres thick. During quiet warm periods in spring the shallow waters at the margin of the lake can be seen to be quite turbid with suspended salt crystals. The thin crusts which ultimately form each year are predominantly rock salt (halite), with minor amounts of magnesium salts. Until recently the salts were dredged from the exposed surface of the main lake and piled up in large heaps at the eastern end, but increasing pollution has brought a halt (in 1991) to the commercial operation. It will be interesting to see how the sedimentation in the lakes evolves if salt layers are not removed in the future.

It is now worthwhile examining the lithified rocks forming the low bluff adjacent to the old road, because they are formed of very fossiliferous Pleistocene shelly deposits including about 2m of iron-shot sands. These appear to be part of the barrier complex in the sense of being a solid 'backbone' against which the unconsolidated younger sands and gravels were piled . Many species of marine bivalves and gastropods are present in the sediments. The upper level of the sequence is secondarily cemented by calcite (calcretised) to form a very hard capping (havara) and contains fossils such as *Pecten* and *Glycimeris* which are very well preserved, but difficult to remove.

Walk across the old road onto the lakeside beach and some 20m out from the edge (water levels permitting) you will pick-up further outcrops of the Pleistocene beds carrying the colonial coral *Cladocora caespitosa*, tubes of the annelid worm *Serpula* and bivalves. The surfaces are commonly scattered with shells, more especially small turreted gastropods. These, and originally loose lake edge sediment, are sporadically cemented to the underlying Pleistocene beds by calcite precipitated from the warm lake waters, forming beach-rock. This process is quite distinct from calcretisation although the final products can be quite similar (see page 93).

14. LAYIA

Location. Sheet 19, K717 Series, 1:50,000. 16km NW of Khirokitia, junction 14
A1 or 10km due WSW of Pano Lefkara (Figure 32). From the latter take the
road leading off the E105 to Kato Dhrys. En route to Layia you pass close to the
15th century Ayios Minas convent noted for its icon painting and its honey (1).
The convent is closed for 3 hours from mid-day and all day Saturday. The
exposures are about 500m NW of Layia (2) (225563) in a road cutting on the
F112, 200m beyond a roadside peg indicating Ora 8km. The road is well
metalled and parking is easy at the beginning of the cutting, adjacent to the road
sign indicating bends ahead.

Summary. This site excellently exposes a range of late Cretaceous volcaniclastic
(mainly epiclastic) sediments, representative of the Transform Sedimentary
Sequences of the Limassol Forest transform fault zone. The site is located along
the axis of the Arakapas Fault Belt (or Zone)

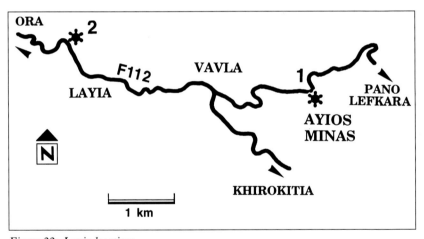

Figure 32: Layia locations.

On both sides of the cutting are exposed a variety of sediments overlain by
pillow lavas, all laid down in just one of several linear fault-controlled submarine
depressions (or grabens) created on the surface of the Troodos and Limassol
Forest ophiolite masses during and after their emplacement. This particular east-
west trending fault belt has a recognisable width of at least 1.5km and is one of
the major structural features of Cyprus. It is referred to as the Arakapas
Transform Fault Belt (or Zone), and it forms the northern boundary of a much
wider transform zone of faulting which encompasses the bulk of the Limassol
Forest ophiolite. A transform fault zone marks the boundary between two

adjacent rock masses when they slide sideways past each other during plate movements. Movement along the Arakapas Belt has brought into contact the diabases of the Sheeted Dyke Complex on the northern side against gabbroic and other Plutonic Complex rocks, including serpentinites, on the southern side. The fault belt outcrops eastwards from this locality for 3km before it becomes covered by younger undeformed sedimentary rocks and westwards via Arakapas village for at least 30km, again being eventually obscured by a younger cover of sediments. (The Arakapas sector of the fault belt is examined again in the Limassol Forest itinerary – see p. 76). There is no reason to doubt that it continues beneath those sediments for some distance and probably all the way along the southern flank of the Troodos mass.

At this locality, and on its approaches from east or west, the Arakapas Fault Belt is marked by a rugged topographic trough. It is very clearly defined on satellite photographs and on the ground and it is interesting to reflect that the present day west-east depression must resemble closely that existing on the surface of the ophiolite during late Cretaceous times. The fill of the trough reaches 500m in thickness in places and consists of mildly metamorphosed (zeolite and greenschist facies) pillow lavas intercalated with wedges of unfossiliferous breccias, sandstones and mudstones. All these form part of what is known as the Transform Sequence and a representative succession is exposed in the road cutting. The fragmentary materials constituting the sedimentary rocks were all derived from altered basalts, diabases or, occasionally, gabbros which outcropped within the fault zone. They are therefore predominantly epiclastic in origin, eroded from adjacent topographic highs on the sea bottom. Curiously, no serpentinite fragments have been found suggesting that that rock was not exposed on the sea bottom at the time of the infilling.

From near to the road sign work your way down the succession for the next 90m or so. The brown-weathered lava flow, of which about 5m is exposed, shows very good pillow structures and rests with very sharp contact on the underlying volcaniclastics, which dip at 30° to the east. There is a thin pale grey-green chilled margin at its base. When the geochemistry of the lava flows is examined they prove to be basaltic in composition with silica percentages between 50-53%, but with a higher magnesia content and greater richness in rare earth elements than the basalt lavas within the Pillow Lava Series of the main Troodos mass. They comprise olivine, orthopyroxene, clinopyroxene and altered glassy feldspathic material, the last caused by rapid cooling in the sea water. This variety of basaltic rock (boninitic in type) seems to be characteristic of transform faults in many parts of the world. The magma appears to have been generated by the partial melting at moderate depths of harzburgite-type rocks and reached the surface relatively easily along the fault planes.

The 5m of sediments below the lava flow are red, iron-rich, well-stratified and worthy of very close inspection (Figure 33). They consist of individual beds of

Figure 33: Tuffaceous sediments. The scale bar (in centimetres) is at the pebbly base of a lighter coloured fining upwards graded bed. The bottom of the succeeding graded bed is marked by a thin, lighter coloured zone.

submarine tuff, up to a metre or more in thickness, each of which grades upwards from a coarse base with small pebbles to a fine grained laminated siltstone or mudstone top. Ripple marks and convolutions affect the laminated layers. The individual constituents of the beds are all of volcanic (including

Figure 34: Epiclastic scree breccias carrying distorted 'rafts' of laminated tuffs. Scale in centimetres.

hydrothermal) origin and were probably mainly eroded from the flanks of the depressions. The manner of emplacement is interesting as it appears to have been by the rapid movement of turbid clouds of loose ash down bottom slopes, a kind of turbidity current mechanism. This conclusion is borne out, not only by the fining-upwards or vertical grading in the deposits but also by the very sharp erosional basal contacts of each bed. At the end of each episode of deposition there was a spell of very quiet settling-out of the finest mud materials and some of these might have been added to by an inwards drift of particles emitted from adjacent hot water (hydrothermal) springs. As the fault zone would be very seismically active at the time the probability is that earth tremors triggered-off the turbidity currents.

The graded tuffs then pass downwards into spectacular scree-like epiclastic breccio-conglomerates, some 12m or more in thickness, where bedding would be difficult to pick out were it not for the occasional intercalation of thin, discontinuous lenses of fine grained tuff (Figure 34). Within the jumbled angular debris there are large slabs, some near vertical some overturned, of lava and other basic igneous rocks. It is likely that the submarine scree deposits were remobilised and moved en-masse sometimes in the form of debris flows down the axes of the troughs. This style of movement could account for the overturning of some of the slabs you see here. Again, all this material has been derived from the flanks of the depressions and, probably, even from occasional transverse ridges built up across them.

Before you leave the cutting note the deep depression on the west side cut into the volcanic sequence and now occupied by about 8m of recent breccia.

15. LIMASSOL FOREST

Location. Sheet 19, K717 Series, 1:50,000. This circular tour starts at Akrounda (Akrounta) (075472) reached by taking the F128 Yermasoyia (Germasogeia) road at junction 24 on the A1 motorway. It continues northwards to Dhierona and Arakapas (102559), eastwards to Ephtagonia (Eftagonia) (145562), then turns southwards along the E109 to Parekklisha (Parekklisia) and the A1 motorway (Figure 35). The road is metalled all the way, but is too narrow and twisting for large tourist coaches.

Summary. The tour is designed to illustrate the transform fault zone structure, some of the main plutonic rock types and the serpentinite shear zones which characterise the Limassol Forest ophiolite, and the boninite-type basaltic lavas of the Arakapas Fault Belt (or Zone).

Note: This tour can be readily combined with the Yermasoyia (Germasogeia) Road itinerary and, in effect, is an extension of it (see p. 131). If time is an important factor it is better to travel to the first exposures in the Limassol Forest ophiolite on the northwestern outskirts of Akrounda village.

Limassol Forest is a complex late Cretaceous ophiolitic mass composed of an elevated east-west core of serpentinitised ultrabasic rocks flanked by a discontinuous envelope of other plutonic rocks and, in the east, Lower Pillow Lavas. It essentially comprises two major groups of igneous rocks. Those formed during sea-floor spreading, referred to as the Axis Sequence, and those formed during intensive fault movements of a transform character, referred to as the Transform Sequence.

On its northern margin the mass is bounded by the east-west trending Arakapas Fault Belt or Zone, which separates it from the Troodos ophiolite, and on its southern and southwestern side it is bounded by the Yersas Fold and Fault Belt or Zone, where it is in contact with younger disturbed sedimentary strata. The discontinuity of structure of the Axis Sequence plutonic rocks, which are mainly layered gabbros, but include serpentinised harzburgite and masses of the Sheeted Dyke Complex (see p. 10), has evoked much comment over the years. The commonly held view is that many of these rocks were displaced upwards, and even partly rotated, as independent masses within serpentinised bodies during their diapiric emplacement, initiated during the original transform deformation. Diapiric describes the upwards intrusion of less dense materials through overlying more dense rock. The mobilised serpentinite, formed hydrothermally by heated sea-waters reacting with ultrabasic harzburgites at depth, appears to have intruded along a very wide east-west trending zone of fracturing and brecciation of which the Arakapas Fault Belt is simply the northern margin. Intrusion appears to have been episodic, one phase occurring before the extrusion on to the sea bottom of the Lower Pillow Lavas, another in later Miocene times. The latter episode probably played some role in the

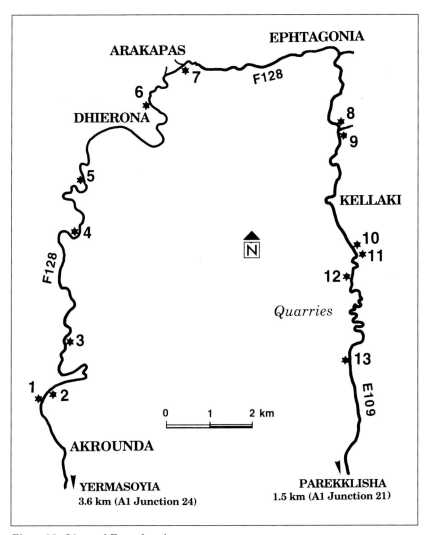

Figure 35: Limassol Forest locations.

deformation seen along the Yerasa Fault and Fold Belt (see p. 102). Several of the later fault movements in the Limassol Forest were along the lines of original east-west trending strike-slip faults running through the ophiolite and are associated with the anticlockwise rotation and obduction of the 'Cyprus Microplate'.

Travel northwestwards out of Akrounda for about 500m to just beyond the football pitch (1). A dirt track forks off acutely to the left at 072478 and for the first 100m or so very good basaltic pillow lavas (Transform Sequence) are intermittently exposed on the right hand side. There then follows a series of occasionally quarried outcrops of faulted and sheared igneous epiclastic debris flow and scree deposits. Epiclastic means that the rock fragments were derived from the erosion of pre-existing igneous rocks exposed, in this case, on the sea floor in late Cretaceous times. The fragments consist of very dark coloured (with a tinge of green due to the presence of chlorite) ultrabasic rocks, such as wehrlites, and light coloured more acid rocks rich in feldspars, such as plagiogranite. These kinds of deposits are a characteristic feature of the Limassol Forest ophiolite mass and recur time and time again throughout its full extent. Continue along the track around a sweeping bend until you see the beginning of a concreted length. The rocks on your right have now changed their character completely and consist of serpentinised harzburgite. About 20m of well jointed but badly broken-up rock are exposed. The serpentinised rock occupies what is referred to as a shear zone. Here, it is about 100m wide and is trending roughly eastwest, which is the typical tectonic fabric of the region. Shear zones, some up to 500m in width and several kilometres in length elsewhere in the ophiolite, are indicated by a prominent near-vertical schistose fabric expressive of very powerful fault movements and deformation pressures, initiated during early transform movements.

Returning to the main road there are two more exposures of sheared serpentinite (2) to be seen by travelling about 250m and 1km (079486) further along it. Along the twisting road leading northwards outcrops are virtually continuous all the way to Dhierona. For approximately the first 5km the ascending road skirts the western flank of a major body of harzburgite also passing through dunites and other ultrabasic igneous rocks of the Axis Sequence together with more shear zones occupied by schistose serpentinite. A vertical contact between harzburgite and brown weathered dunite, carrying serpentinite veins, is well exposed 3km from Akrounda (077492) at a sharp right hand bend with a narrow parking space opposite overlooking the deeply entrenched valley to the west (3). This contact is of more than passing interest as it marks what is known as 'The Petrological Moho', the boundary between mantle rocks, represented by the harzburgite, and crustal rocks represented by the dunites.

The road eventually passes over gabbroic rocks before sweeping upwards and eastwards to reach a very distinct col located on a broad left-hand bend of the road, some 8.5km from Akrounda (4) (083518). There is ample parking on the side of the road facing the outcrop and there are splendid views southwards across the deeply dissected scrubbily vegetated terrain with its overlapping spurs to the sea.

Figure 36: Picrite (P) and werhlite dykes intruded into harzburgite (H). The section runs west to east.

The exposure comprises a number of impressive ultrabasic, picritic dyke-like bodies which belong to the Transform Sequence and are intruded into the ultrabasic Axis Sequence of the Limassol Forest ophiolite (Figure 36). The picritic bodies are younger than the Axis Sequence and were emplaced during some of the phases of acute faulting associated with the massive internal dislocation of the ophiolite. All this illustrates the complex structure and ongoing evolution of the Axis Sequence during Cretaceous times. The bodies dip at about 50° southeastwards and are picked out by changes in coloration. Low-angled faults dipping to the left run across the lower part of the face. The easiest rocks to identify are olivine-rich picrite dykes which have very prominent grey, fine grained chilled margins up to 10cm wide. The dykes also exhibit crude close-spaced cooling joints internally, at right angles to their margins. The inference is that they were intruded into host rocks which must have been cold at the time. These host rocks are serpentinised harzburgite and werhlite. In reality it is quite a challenge working out which is which between these two as the rocks are variably weathered, although the serpentinised harzburgite usually has a light grey sheen and occurs as solid masses. There is such a mass immediately above the most easterly fault plane where the fault dips below the road surface. Werhlite is a coarse grained brown-weathering plutonic rock consisting of olivine and pyroxene and occurs as intrusions into the harzburgite, though there are no chilled margins to emphasise and locate the contacts. The harzburgite must have still been hot when the wehrlite was emplaced.

The next location is exactly 3km further on (087532) and is a spectacular cross-section through yet another east-west trending serpentinite shear zone, this time a major one with a width of about 500m (5). The 60m long exposure on the southside (left) of the road, with ample parking opposite, exhibits highly contorted and foliated schists, some almost talc-like in composition.

Now carry on via Dhierona and Arakapas. Just north of Dhierona there are splendid views across the Arakapas Fault Belt or Zone into Troodos ophiolite country. Keep an eye out for an array of dykes well exposed in the innumerable road cuttings leading down into Arakapas village (6). They are predominantly doleritic in composition, though now slightly altered, and belong to the Sheeted Dyke Complex.

Take the new bypass on the south side of the village, heading eastwards. Some 500m onwards, on the right hand side of the road to Ephtagonia (Eftagonia), basaltic lavas outcrop showing excellent pillow structure (7) (107558). These were extruded along the Arakapas Fault Belt. The pillows exhibit green glassy rinds indicative of rapid cooling and alteration of the glass into clay minerals by sea water, and sometimes have 'bread-crust' surfaces and gas cavities (vesicles) at their margins. Chert, a sedimentary siliceous rock, is present in between the pillows in places. The chemistry of the lavas differs from that of the basic lavas constituting the Upper and Lower Pillow Lavas in the Troodos ophiolite sequence in being richer in magnesia and light rare earth elements, such as zirconium and hafnium. The lava appears to be a special variety of glassy basalt, having affinities with a rock known as boninite, and owes its fundamental nature to magma generated from the partial melting of harzburgite beneath transform fault zones. The highly fractured zone probably allowed the magma to exit from depth more easily compared with lavas of the 'normal' Pillow Lava Series, so the cooling history was different. (See Layia, p. 68).

The road from Arakapas to Ephtagonia is essentially along this west-east belt, which existed as a closely parallel series of faulted deep-sea troughs with rugged relief during the formation of the ophiolites. In these narrow troughs the basaltic lavas poured forth and there they intermingled with scree-like breccias, sands and finer grained muds, all originating from ophiolitic rocks exposed along the flanks and within the troughs (see p. 69). (The lavas are very well exposed along the roadside). The association of rocks of detrital origin is commonly referred to as the Transform Sedimentary Sequence and is well developed along the lengths or axes of the fault-controlled depressions.

On the southern outskirts of Ephtagonia turn southwards onto the E109 leading to Kellaki and ultimately to Parekklisha. Travel up the rising twisting road for about 2km, roughly halfway to Kellaki, where you will find ample exposures within the Sheeted Dyke Complex (8) (145545). 500m further on, and just after a small bridge cutting obliquely across the road, there are exposures of light coloured plagiogranite on the east side of the road which appear to have been intruded into the Sheeted Dyke Complex (9). Hereabouts, on the southern side of the main fault zone depression, the outcrop of the Complex is about 10km east-west and about 3km north-south.

Kellaki village is situated on a large outcrop of mainly gabbros and about 1.5km and 2km south of it occur good roadside exposures. 500m south of the Manolas Tavern at 149515 (10) there is a good 3m high exposure and if you walk down the road for about 150m plagiogranite dykes and veins appear once more. The gabbros are generally highly weathered, but show evidence of alteration at some early stage in their history as the pyroxenes of the original rock have been changed into secondary hornblende (uralite), which is often fibrous in habit.

There are many basic dykes cutting through the rocks. A good example occurs a little further down the road where it swings sharply to the right (149512) (11). A 30cm dyke cuts through a pyroxenite and is truncated by yet another fault or shear zone, about 2m wide, occupied by sheared serpentinite.

750m further south (12) (147508) occurs a really spectacular section through gabbros of the layered variety, indicative of an originally lower level within the ophiolite sequence (Figure 37). The exposures are where a very sharp bend in the original road has been cut-off and there is ample parking space at the

Figure 37: Tilted layered gabbros (G) intruded by light coloured plagiogranite dykes (P).

southern end of the cut-off. The layering approaches the vertical in many places and strikes roughly northwest-southeast. The individual layers are variable in thickness and show up because of slight differences in the proportions of plagioclase feldspars and dark brown-weathering ferro-magnesian minerals. The presence of light coloured plagiogranite dyke-like intrusions paralleling the layering also makes this outcrop very interesting and a subject for debate.

From this point the ground falls away to the south and on a clear day the splendid view encompasses the lower lying ground immediately to the south formed initially of a wide outcrop of the Lower Pillow Lavas, with Parekklisha (Parekklisia) village and its by-pass visible, then a narrow low-lying strip occupied by the Moni Melange (see p. 102) and finally, nearing the sea, the north-facing escarpments of the Lefkara and Pakhna Formations. Immediately to the front are large active working quarries in the diabases of the Sheeted Dyke Complex. The material is suitable for aggregate purposes. The quarries are also near the site of the abortive Pevkos Prospect, explored in the 1950's for copper, iron, cobalt and nickel disseminations in a zone which extended for more than 600m in a north-westerly direction.

Continue down the winding road until it begins to flatten out. Just before you reach the second entrance to the quarry complex, owned by Skyramont Quarries Ltd, and against a galaxy of roadside notices indicating bends and a 13 per cent gradient there are good 10m high exposures on the west side of the road of some of the rocks being worked in the adjacent quarries (147488) (13). Between the quarry entrance and a few tens of metres beyond the kilometre post is the Basal Group (lavas intruded by dykes) and this is faulted against the Sheeted Dyke Complex to the north. The dykes are very well exposed, often showing cross-cutting relationships and good chilled margins. They dip at 45° to the south.

Now continue via the Parekklisha by-pass back to the A1 motorway.

16. MARGI (MARKI)

Location. Sheet 12, K717 Series, 1:50,000. 16km due south-southwest of Nicosia. Turn west off the A1 motorway at junction 7 onto the E102 road, labelled Kochati or travel out of Nicosia on the E901 road to Xeri and fork off to the left 2.5km south of that large village (Figure 38). Grid reference 293754.

Summary. This site is characterised by late Cretaceous umber deposits resting on basic and ultrabasic pillow lavas of the uppermost part of the Troodos ophiolite, with associated volcanic vents.

Where the Xeri (Tseri) to Kochati metalled road eventually turns sharply to the east follow the lead-off road to the west into Margi (1) village, a very small agglomeration of houses and farm buildings. Turn southwards onto a dirt track

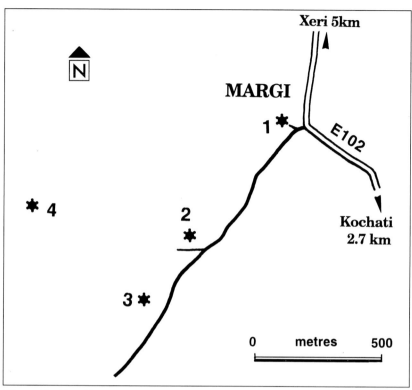

Figure 38: Margi locations.

and follow this for about 800m. The bumpy track is suitable for small coaches and 4-wheel drive vehicles only. Ordinary cars should park at the village.

The Margi area is crossed by a series of north-south striking faults cutting through the Middle Lefkara Formation white chalks (Palaeocene) and underlying black, grey and red Upper Pillow Lavas, which form the top of the late Cretaceous Troodos ophiolite. These faults lead to a repetition in outcrop, and this is reflected in the north-south grain to the topography. The track cuts obliquely across the grain. The first objective is a very prominent upstanding mass (2) on the northern side of the track consisting of an intrusive body formed to a large extent of an ultrabasic igneous rock, known as a picrite. Picrites are very dark olivine- and augite-rich rocks carrying a little plagioclase feldspar, and in the Margi area the fresh-looking green olivine grains are commonly very prominent. They were derived from the melting of ultrabasic rocks in the deeper parts of the ophiolite complex, probably harzburgite or peridotite. Although there has been some controversy about this particular outcrop it has every appearance of a volcanic plug occupying a small vent or pipe cutting through the lava pile and through which later lavas were poured out onto adjacent irregularities on the sea bed. It is claimed that as you trace the mass down the slopes to the east it passes eastwards into a massive basic sheet flow and ultimately into a pillowed lava. Walk up the stable scree slope at the foot of the steep southern face of the outcrop to inspect the pillow lavas at the base through which the vent was cut. The lavas are shot through with secondary carbonate veins. The intrusive darker-looking plug is also veined, but additionally shows strong near-horizontal jointing, undoubtedly created during the cooling of the hot plug materials.

An easy scramble up to the top of this plug via its eastern flank will enable you to have a splendid view of the surrounding terrain (see back cover, top).

Successive escarpments of the Lefkara chalks, dipping gently to the east at 10-25° stand out well as you look towards the east and you can see that they rest with a very sharp junction on the underlying lavas, which also dip eastwards but at a higher angle of 25-35°. This junction is an angular unconformity, representing a break in deposition probably lasting several hundreds of thousands of years. The irregularity in altitude of the base of the chalks is due in part to the irregular surface of the lavas on which they were deposited and partly due to the subsequent faulting. It is very noticeable that the upper 20m or so of the basaltic, normally grey lavas are pink or red stained. This colouration seems to be due to the subsequent oxidation of very fine grained iron-rich materials, such as sulphides in colloidal form, which filtered down from their suspension in the sea into the top of the lavas, before the chalks were laid down. The view to the north and west encompasses further outcrops of the chalk escarpments, swinging around so that they begin to strike east-west and dip towards the north, and extensive, partly cropped areas with outcrops of lava. Although a rough topography characterises the lavas they do not form high ground.

Some 250m westwards from the picrite plug is a north-south elongated infilled pit (3). On its steep face outcrop brown weathered pillow lavas over which is draped a peculiar chestnut to chocolate-brown deposit, known as umber (Figure 39). Umber is a manganese-bearing iron-rich sediment, extremely fine grained and homogeneous in texture, light in weight and soft. It tends to be concentrated in isolated depressions on the surface of the lavas, more especially around the northern flanks of the Troodos mass. The pockets rarely extend for more than 150m laterally or reach thicknesses of more than 10m. A close inspection of the face in front of you, more especially towards the southern end, reveals the close relationship between the lavas and the overlying deposit, with the umber moulding itself around the pillows and occupying the original cavities between them.

Figure 39: Umber deposits (dark at the top of the face) resting on light coloured weathered pillow lavas.

The origin of these economically valuable deposits is a matter for argument, some authorities believing that they formed by the accumulation of material derived from the slow submarine weathering of the cold lavas, others suggesting that they represent rapidly deposited chemical precipitates laid down adjacent to warm hydrothermal springs emanating from within the still hot lava pile.

Whatever its origin the umber is only a little younger than, or even contemporary with, the last stages of lava eruption and on the basis of faunal evidence within associated radiolarian cherts and clays is late Cretaceous (Campanian) in age. The cherts and clays used to be exposed here but are now covered by fill, though you may still find chert fragments in the spoil. The whole of this sedimentary association is known as the Perapedhi Formation.

If you now follow the track around the southern end of the old pit, you will enter an area characterised by elongated scarp-like features formed by a mixed, almost cyclical succession of basalt and basaltic andesite pillow lava flows and massive sheet flows. The latter usually form the higher ridges as they weather less readily than the pillow lavas. Walk along to the next obvious ridge before diverting off northwards along it. Looking down and around from any high point on the ridge you will observe that some lavas are 'normal' grey in appearance and a few others are distinctly black-looking. The base of certain grey lavas is also black. This black colouration is because the rock is picritic in composition. Large green olivine grains, up to 3cm in size, typify the picrites and their size indicates that many of them were probably forming over a long period of time in the magma chambers at depth before reaching the surface. One probable vent or pipe has already been inspected, but it now worthwhile seeking out any other possible feeder vents from which at least some of the lavas issued forth. One such is located about 350m along the ridge, on its eastern side and just beyond a col-like feature (4). A solitary tree exists some 20m to the north of what appears to be a circular vent (forming a conical mound surrounded by a depression) and associated picritic lava flow. The 3m thick lava flow, pillowed at the top, can be traced for about 20m to the south. It is noticeable that the olivine grains are up to 3cm in size in the axial part of the pipe, but around the periphery decrease to 1-2mm, because of relatively rapid chilling of the magma against the basaltic lavas.

If you look carefully at the lava flow succession hereabouts, you will begin to pick out intercalated thin layers of fine grained, laminated and iron-shot sediment. These dense rocks consist of fine grained calcite in which are dispersed patches of very coarse calcite enclosing highly altered lava fragments. Discrete grains of epidote also occur. These curious carbonate-rich rocks, deposited between successive lava flows, are possibly a consequence of the submarine weathering of the lavas.

17. MARI

Location. Sheet 24, K717 Series, 1:50,000. 25km east of Limassol. Exit 16 off A1 motorway, then travel northeastwards for about 1.5km on the old B1 Limassol-Nicosia road. Access to the large pit, about 600m away, is along a wide flat dirt track leading off to the right (southeast) (Figure 22). Grid reference 269443. Parking is easy.

Summary. This is an interesting exposure exhibiting a sequence of fossiliferous Pleistocene sediments including one of the higher level raised beaches (+25m?) of Cyprus.

The intermittently worked lower part of the pit consists of some 30m of greenish grey-pale brown marls, which are rich in highly comminuted shell debris, including calcareous foraminifera, and have a clay mineral content dominated by mixed layer smectite-chlorite with minor amounts of kaolinite and illite. Thin shelled marine bivalves of the tellin type occur, though rarely. Close inspection of the nearly vertical faces shows that bedding is present and cream coloured stringers emphasise this. There is evidence for bioturbation in the presence of numerous oblique tubes or burrows, up to 2mm wide. A mild degree of faulting is indicated by slickensided faces.

The origin of the marl is conjectural, but it clearly represents relatively quiet deposition, probably in some protected area or basin not subject to intensive wave and current activity. The distinctive clay component may well have been derived directly from the nearby Kannaviou and Moni smectite-rich bentonites, which were probably exposed to marine erosion at the time. The age of the deposit is also conjectural, but is probably early-middle Pleistocene and as such could be a particular localised facies of the Athalassa Formation.

Now walk up the ramp on the left hand side of the pit to inspect the upper part of the sequence, which comprises 20m of younger, unfaulted, light brown, quartz-bearing calcareous sands and gravels. The contact with the underlying marls is sharp and erosive, with minor channelling. Immediately above this contact the sands are laminated, cross-laminated and sometimes carry clay pellets (or galls) indicative of erosive current activity. Detritals include quartz, bleached biotite, green amphiboles and chlorite and a range of highly altered ferromagnesian minerals. Chert acts as a mild cement in places. Decomposed iron-stained land plant debris is widespread and this is intermingled with abundant marine shell fragments, including foraminifera, bryozoa, the shallow water oyster *Ostrea* and the highly turreted gastropod (with a truncated spire) *Truncatella*. Gravel seams and lenses are interleaved with the sands towards the top of the face. The overall character of the deposits suggests that they are much younger than the marls beneath, on which they rest with unconformity. They appear to be part of a raised beach (marine terrace). But which one? The original surveys of the area suggest that it could be the +8-11m late Pleistocene raised beach, as seen along the nearby coastline, but the altitude of the site suggests that it could be the next higher late Pleistocene raised beach at about +25m.

18. MARONI

Location. Sheet 20, K717 Series, 1:50,000. Exits 14 or 15 from A1 motorway. 35km west of Larnaca and 35km east of Limassol (Figure 40). Grid reference 327474.

Summary. This location illustrates the close environmental relationship between the late Miocene Koronia reef limestones and the Kalavasos Formation salt deposits.

Access to the site is via the village of Psematismenos, then forking left (southeast) towards the outskirts of Maroni village. (If you fork right you soon come across the main entrance to some gypsum quarries, where in 1992 active working was taking place. The quarry faces, which are visible from the A1 motorway, are very dangerous and permission to visit is very time-consuming. As all the salient feature of the gypsum beds can be seen equally readily at Maroni, Tokhni and Kalavasos (see pp. 124 and 50) it is much better not to waste time arranging to visit these quarries). Just before the first house at Maroni, and at the beginning of the first left-hand bend, there is a dirt track leading-off uphill to the left (1). Parking is easy. River terrace gravels and sands are exposed in a bluff at the side of the track, and certain of the coarser boulders and pebbles show marked imbrication, like the overlapping of roof-tiles. This is characteristic of

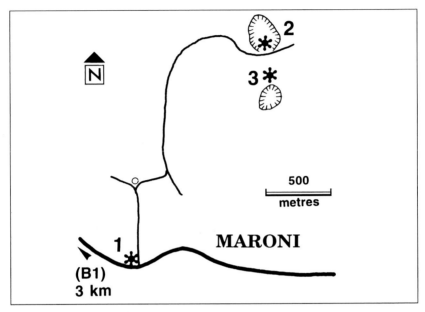

Figure 40: Maroni locations.

these water-laid deposits. Continue along the track, which occasionally deteriorates, northwards until you see the foundations of a circular structure, then fork right until you meet a T-junction, where you turn left. At this point you will be able to see the objective on the facing slope and skyline to the northeast, which is a group of prominent knolls (2). The total walking distance to the knolls from the road is about 2km.

Nearing the knolls, notice that there are exposed in the rising track large pockets of crystalline, sugary-textured gypsum, very white in appearance. In the rather rubbly-looking field below the track there are even more extensive patches outcropping, and it is worthwhile spending some time looking for the different varieties of gypsum, not only the sugary type but also creamy, very fine grained alabaster and clear transparent and well-formed bladed crystals of secondary selenite. Many of the last are several centimetres in length and show a swallow-tail twinned structure. At the trackside adjacent to the uppermost knoll you will also see an excellent 'rosette' (concretion) formed of radiating blades of selenite and again caused by secondary recrystallisation with the original salt deposits (Figure 41). There are many such in the shallow quarries below the track. All these salt beds belong to the Kalavasos Formation of Miocene age and were laid down on a shallow water marine shelf in depressions bounded by reefs.

Figure 41: Gypsum rosette. Scale in centimetres.

The limestones forming the knolls, which have been quarried in the past, are also Miocene in age and are part of the Koronia Formation. They are massive and structureless, though brecciated in places. There appears to be an absence of large fossils, but close inspection reveals in places the traces of algal laminae, and it is these which give a clue to the origin of the knolls as algal reef-like mounds generated in clear and shallow seas. The apparent absence of reef colonial corals and other typical reef fauna probably reflects the increasing salinity of the sea water, which eventually led to the precipitation of the Kalavasos gypsum deposits in and around the mounds. It is certain that the reefs ceased growing as soon as high salinities appropriate for gypsum precipitation were reached. If you want to see the close relationship between the salt deposits and the reef limestones

Figure 42: Contact of reef limestones and darker fluted gypsum beds. The scale bar (in centimetres) is at the contact (>).

examine the foot of the western side of the knoll 40m downslope from the track (3). There the gypsum is in direct contact with the reef (Figure 42).

A noticeable feature of the knoll limestones, and particularly well-seen, again in the rugged exposures about 40m downslope from the track, are cavities and secondary veins occupied by a pearly white mineral, celestite (strontium sulphate). This mineral was probably precipitated from circulating pore fluids moving through the reefs and extracting strontium from the calcareous algae, which are enriched in this element during life.

19. MATHIATI COPPER MINE

Location. Sheet 20, K717 Series, 1:50,000. 25km south of Nicosia via the A1 motorway, exiting at junction 8 and continuing via Perakhorio and Ayia Varvara on the E103 (Figure 43). Grid reference 317707.

Summary. This is a spectacular abandoned copper mine showing the method of working of the orebody, which is located at the junction of the Lower and very well-exposed Upper Pillow Lavas of the Troodos ophiolite. Ochres are well-developed.

Note: A visit to this mine is worth considering in conjunction with a visit to Sha mine, some 6km away by road via Mathiatis village (see p .108).

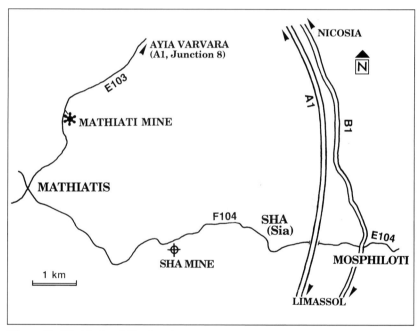

Figure 43: Mathiati and Sha locations.

The deep opencast mine is located 3km from Ayia Varvara on the east side of the road (1) (Figure 44). It is marked by vast slag heaps, though the large pit with its classical inverted cone shape and spiral access roads only becomes visible when you park immediately above it. There is abundant parking space near to the decaying mine buildings. The mine was opened up in the 1930's, but major mining operations of the proved 3 million ton massive sulphide ore (a comparatively small amount) only started in 1965. Work has been intermittent over the last few years and on a small scale, but effectively ceased in about 1987. Since then the pit has become flooded to nearly half of its full depth. There seem to be no problems regarding access to the lowest visible levels, but clearly great care needs to be exercised at all times. If you do not wish to descend into the mine there is some very good collecting that can be done in the spoil heaps perched on the rim, adjacent to the parking area.

Figure 44: Overview of Mathiati mine.

The cupriferous ore bodies of Cyprus are generally confined to the upper levels of the Lower Pillow Lavas and are overlain by unmineralised Upper Pillow Lavas. The mineralisation, therefore, pre-dates the extrusion of the Upper Pillow Lavas. There is one major exception to this generality and that is at Skouriotissa to the north of Mount Olympus, where the orebody occurs at the top of the UPL (see p. 109). Pyrites and the more silvery-looking marcasite are the dominant primary sulphides in all the deposits, with minor amounts of copper pyrites (chalcopyrites) associated with traces of gold and silver. The main secondary minerals, producing by secondary enrichment and leaching processes, include copper-bearing chalcocite, covellite and bornite. Despite the attention paid to copper in Cyprus travel and holiday publications the percentage of copper in the ore bodies only ranges up to 5 per cent and at Mathiati is only about 0.3 per cent.

All the sulphide ore bodies of Cyprus are associated with zones of intense faulting and fracturing and it is probable that these zones enabled the mineralising fluids to escape upwards. The original form of the main ore body here, as elsewhere, was lensoid or saucer-shaped, but subsequent faulting has led to truncation at the northeastern and southwestern end of the pit. Nonetheless, as the form roughly parallels the surfaces of the associated lava flows the bodies are said to be stratiform. The shape of the bodies suggests that they accumulated in small depressions on the Lower Pillow Lavas surface as a consequence of localised upwards-streaming of sea water, heated to temperatures of about 350 °C by passage through the lava pile and basic plutonic rocks at depth. These streams of hot gaseous and acid fluid, rich in leached metals from the underlying igneous rocks, possibly emerged at the bottom of the sea as hot springs or gushers, building up chimney-like structures in doing so; these are known as 'black smokers'. The fluids then reacted with the cooler alkaline sea water and primary sulphides were precipitated onto the sea floor. The passage upwards of hot mineralising fluids is indicated by the structure of the ore body at depth. Beneath the main massive and partially conglomeratic ore level, now worked out here, is a hydrothermally altered zone containing mainly pyrites and silica in the form of quartz, chalcedony and chert. This passes downwards into a brecciated and highly altered stockwork carrying varying amounts of sulphide minerals, usually between pillows or in fractures in pillows. Stockworks in these situations extend downwards for several hundred of metres. All these levels have been productive in their time, depending on economic conditions.

As you begin to walk down the dirt track to the present bottom of the pit note on the right hand side the splendid pillow structures in the basalt and basaltic andesite Upper Pillow Lavas. Some of the pillows are as much as a metre and a half across, and you will not see any finer examples in Cyprus. Thin films and patches of the white zeolite analcite are present throughout. All the time you are descending you will be conscious of the yellowish-brown coloured, tumbled southeastern wall of the pit. This, on close inspection (look at fallen blocks) proves to be ochre, a fine grained aggregate of hydrous iron oxides, more especially goethite. Within it are grains and blocks of pyrites and quartz, and traces of gold and silver. There is little doubt that the ochre is genetically connected with the ore body and the consensus is that it represents a sub-aqueous oxidation and leaching of the upper part of that body, when it was exposed on the sea floor. This oxidation, producing what is sometimes known as a gossan, must have occurred during a pause in the eruption of the lava pile because the Upper Pillow Lavas are totally unaffected. At some other ochre localities, but not here, lamination and bedding can be seen in the ochres, indicating a partial reworking and redistribution of the oxides by bottom currents.

Continue further down the track, noting the good vertical columnar jointing caused by cooling in a sheet lava flow some way up the eastern face, then deviate onto one of horizontal levels, just above the water-line. Here, you are virtually within the stockwork zone of the ore body. Although the scattered loose blocks have been well picked-over, a close inspection will invariably find veins and surfaces carrying ore minerals. The glassy and pearly zeolite heulandite can be found in small patches in these highly altered members of the Lower Pillow Lavas.

Finally, if you want to inspect a very small exposure of umber, an iron-manganese deposit associated with the upper surfaces of pillow lavas, turn right out of the parking area and continue eastwards along the main road for about 100m. On the right hand side of the road the slightly overgrown brown coloured deposits are readily accessible (see p. 80).

20. PANO LEFKARA

Location. Sheet 20, K717 Series. 1:50,000. 45km from Limassol, 55km from Nicosia. The E105 access road, leading off from the A1 motorway is much improved as far as the southern outskirts of Pano Lefkara (Figure 45).

Summary. Exposures in the Middle Lefkara Formation calci-turbidite chalks at its type locality.

The exposures to be visited (1 & 2) are located close to the T-junction with the Kato Dhrys – Ayios Minas Monastery road which leads off to the left (south); the junction overlooks Kato (Lower) Lefkara village. A cafe is conveniently located at this splendid northwards-facing viewing point (286575). Here, you are standing on Palaeocene Middle Lefkara Formation chalks and

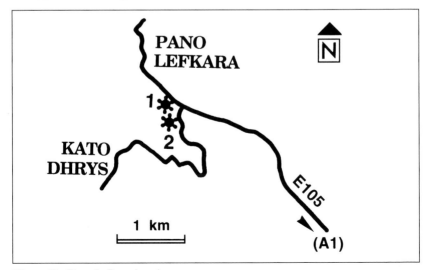

Figure 45: Pano Lefkara locations.

marls, which dip gently to the southeast. The ground falls away to the two Lefkara villages, Upper (Pano) to the west and Lower (Kato) to the front, which are also built on Lefkara Formation chalks. Then, in the middle distance is the looming southern edge of the eastern extremity of the main Troodos ophiolite mass, here comprising low relief pillow lavas and higher relief, peaky sheeted dykes, but also intermittently faced by a mantle of more fertile, grass-covered scree. Some of the scree deposits are said to extend beneath the unconformable cover of the Lefkara chalks. If this is so, it signifies that the surface of the ophiolite mass, hereabouts, underwent extensive submarine weathering and disintegration prior to the onset of chalk deposition. On a clear day, through gaps in the ophiolite range, can be seen Lefkara Formation chalks, in the vicinity of Margi, 19km away, but this time they are dipping away to the north (see p. 78).

The attractive, very photogenic red roofscape, reasonably well preserved mediaeval houses and the white facade of the Church of the Holy Cross of Pano Lefkara reminds us that this was a former summer resort for the Venetian aristocracy. For centuries it has been the home for needle-made lace, based on linen, and it is reported that Leonardo da Vinci acquired lace here for the altar cloth of Milan Cathedral in 1481. Silverware, some locally produced, is also in marked evidence in the innumerable shops. Parking is not easy in Pano Lefkara in summer.

The roadside exposures (1) leading away down the sloping main road for about 300m, tend to deteriorate as time goes by due to frost shattering in winter and soil creep. Nonetheless, they remain sufficiently instructive, especially if loose material is also looked at closely. The *in situ* Lefkara chalks and marls are thinly bedded and carry thin films and lenticles of secondary chert. The deposits are the lithified equivalents of pelagic calcareous oozes, probably laid down in one of the relatively deep depressions existing on the surface of the late Cretaceous Cyprus ophiolites. The position of the nearest depression at the time might have been along the Arakapas Transform Fault Belt (see p. 7) which runs west-east 3km to the south, and was an original topographic depression formed between the Troodos and Limassol Forest ophiolitic masses. The ooze appears to have been intermittently re-mobilised and transported down the flanks of the depression by small scale turbidity currents, hence some of the beds can be referred to as calci-turbidites. They are indicated by a bed becoming finer grained upwards, a feature not easy with the naked eye, but more apparent with a hand lens. The base is likely to have a fine sand- or silt-grade texture and this changes upwards into a very fine grained mud-grade (lutite) texture. Cross-lamination, again on a small scale, can be picked-up in the upper parts of a given bed. This has proved useful in determining the broad direction of flow of the turbidity currents, and detailed work has indicated a dominantly northwest to southeast movement. Pauses in sedimentation allowed the temporary colonisation of the oozes by a range of soft-bodied burrowing organisms, and fine tube-like traces of one such, *Chondrites*, can be found, most easily in loose fragments at the foot of the exposures.

If you want to examine rather fresher faces in these chalks travel southwards for about 250m along the Kato Dhrys road, where recent road widening has produced some good exposures (2) (286573).

21. PAPHOS (PAFOS) AIRPORT

Location. Sheet 22, K717 Series, 1:50,000. 12km southeast of Paphos (Figure 46). Grid reference 532412. Take the E603 Airport access road, leading southwards from the main Paphos-Limassol B6 coastal road.

Summary. This locality is one of the best in southern Cyprus for modern beachrock, resting on disturbed ?Pliocene-Pleistocene deposits.

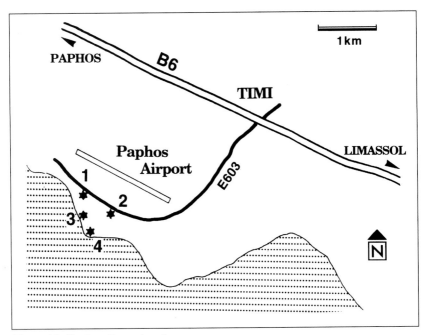

Figure 46: Paphos Airport locations.

Follow the airport access road as far as the terminal buildings and hangars on its south side, where there is ample parking space (1). The airport was opened in 1983. A pleasant and protected spot for a picnic is the specially laid out grove of eucalyptus trees by the side of the road, 400m short of the buildings (2).

From the airport parking area take the dirt road leading southwards towards
the low-cliffed headland and adjacent beach, some 400m away (3). Initially, the
beach is pebbly with a wide range of loose materials derived from local sources,
such as the Pakhna Formation and Pleistocene raised beaches (marine terraces),
and from more distant ophiolite sources. Pebbles from the latter, being relatively
hard basic igneous rocks, tend to predominate, even though they must have
passed through a very complex history of recycling from one deposit to another,
before reaching their present beach resting place. The fascinating feature here,
however, is the splendid development of a metre or so of thinly and lenticularly
bedded beach-rock, extending from just below mean low water mark to well
above mean high water mark (Figure 47). Beach-rock has been described at
other locations in this Guide (see p. 64), but none compare in scale with what
you see here. The individual layers seem to have 'fossilised' the beach profile, in
the sense that they dip gently down towards low water mark, matching the
surface topography of the original unlithified beach. The cementing materials for
the pebbles are aragonite and calcite, both varieties of calcium carbonate, and
these have been, and continue to be, precipitated from carbonate-rich warm sea
water splashing over onto the beach, and from circulating groundwater. The
width of the beach-rock zone, 15m or so, probably reflects the degree of wave-
splash during strong onshore wind conditions. If beach-rock could be preserved
and dated from any included fossils then it clearly could give a pointer towards

Figure 47: Beach rock.

assessing the position of mean high water mark at the time it formed. This information would be useful in regions of small tidal range, such as Cyprus, for determining sea-level changes.

Head for the small cliff, formed of more consolidated, well bedded calcareous sands and silts dipping at about 10° towards the southwest (4). These deposits are possibly Pleistocene in age, maybe equivalent to the Athalassa Formation in other parts of the island, or are Pliocene (Nicosia Formation). The sands are highly calcareous, cross-bedded and lenticular, and are variably calcreted. If you now traverse eastwards for a hundred metres you will come across further examples of beach-rock backed by exposures of very strongly jointed sands with dips up to 18° in a northeasterly direction. The disoriented beds with their nearly vertical joints are concentrated in a zone about 60m wide, which suggests some fundamental and probably deep-seated cause for its location. Maybe Pleistocene or later movements of a deep-seated fault in the ophiolite basement created localised stresses in the cover deposits sufficient to generate this anomalous zone. Could there be some relationship to the repeated earthquakes which have afflicted the Paphos area, especially in the fourth century?

22. PETOUNDA POINT

Location. Sheet 20, K717 Series, 1:50,000. 18km WSW of Larnaca and 3km due S of Mazotos (Figure 48). Grid reference 452487.

Summary. This location has excellent exposures in highly disturbed, slumped Upper Lefkara Formation chalks, which are capped by very fossiliferous calcreted +11m Pleistocene Raised Beach deposits.

A network of dirt tracks leads southwards from Mazotos village, but probably the easiest access route to follow is via the acute road junction leading off the tarmac Kiti coastal road about 1.5km east of Mazotos. The dirt track leading off westwards is very wide here and continues as such until the final turn-off to the south after about 1.5km (449505). This turn-off is on to a very narrow track, unsuitable for a wide coach, and marked by a solitary pine tree carrying one old notice board. You will know if you are on the correct track by seeing in front of you the dome of a beautiful small church. About 200m before the church the track forks to the left (southeastwards) and carries on beyond some farm buildings. You can now see the site of the old gravel workings at the headland to the south, and those are what you are heading for and where you can easily park (1). You are now located at the eastern end of the Petounda Point promontory.

The route is along the pebbly beach and around the first headland, for a distance of about 400m. The beach is initially narrow, quite safe, but there is likely to be a mild degree of scrambling around and over large fallen blocks from the cliff face, which is very susceptible to slipping and sliding. The cliff here is

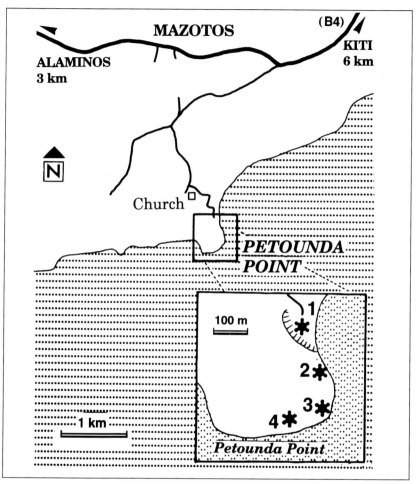

Figure 48: Petounda Point locations.

predominantly formed of Upper Lefkara Formation (Oligocene) white chalks carrying pronounced red haematitised laminae, capped by 2-3m of late Pleistocene Raised Beach (or marine terrace) deposits. The regional dip of these chalk beds is low and of the order of 5-15° to the south and southeast, but at this particular locality something very strange seems to have happened. This is first noticeable some 80m south of the old buildings at the beginning of the cliff section (2) where the laminated chalks are highly contorted and tightly overfolded. Some of the fold structures have a sheath-like aspect with fold axes that are nearly horizontal (Figure 49). Some beds are even vertical in disposition, all these structures being emphasised by fine haematite staining along the laminae and bedding planes. Features of this kind are repeated along the rest of the traverse and a thickness of at least 15m of the chalks is affected. The nature of the distortions suggests that they formed by the slumping of partially lithified,

Figure 49: 'Sheath' folding in iron-stained Lefkara Formation chalks. The horizontal fold is about 1m from left to right.

still plastic, chalky muds down gentle slopes on the sea bottom towards the end of Lefkara times. The direction of movement was probably towards what is now the southeast. Why this displacement should occur is conjectural, but there might have been some major earth tremor, associated with fault movements in the underlying ophiolitic foundation rocks, which triggered it off. It was clearly a regional event as the Lefkara chalks at Cape Kiti, some 11km to the east, were affected in a similar fashion at the same time.

While you are looking at the chalks keep casting your eyes up to the Raised Beach, located at about +11m, which rests with marked discordance on the chalks. In some places the gravels, sands and silts constituting the beach are piped down into the underlying beds. These younger late Pleistocene deposits, dated at about 190,000 years old, are all variably cemented by calcite (calcreted), especially towards the overhanging top, to give a rather rubbly weathered appearance. Several large cemented fallen blocks now reside on or are adjacent to the modern beach and are well worth close inspection (3). The colonial Madreporarian coral *Cladocora caespitosa* is present in some, though it is not always clear if it is in its growth position or was swept onto the late Pleistocene beach from its normal place of growth, which could have been anything between 1-70m below sea-level. There are sponges and numerous large bivalves, such as *Pecten* and *Ostrea*, and a variety of gastropods, including large *Murex*.

At several places along the south-facing tumbled cliff it is possible for the fit to scramble up to the top and walk back, across the strongly calcreted upper surface of the Raised Beach (4), to the car park. Otherwise retrace your steps along the present beach.

23. PETRA TOU ROMIOU

Location. Sheet 22, K717 Series, 1:50,000. 25km east of Paphos, 45km west of Limassol on the main coastal road B6 (Figure 50). Grid reference 659360.

Summary. An excellent introduction to the sedimentary and igneous olistoliths incorporated into the tectonised melange within the late Cretaceous Mamonia Complex.

Note: These exposures in the Mamonia Complex are best done first, before exploring generally more complicated adjacent areas in the Complex (see the Dhiarizos river section, p. 41, and Ayia Varvara, Paphos, p. 28).

The 'Rock of the Roman' is the legendary birthplace of Aphrodite, the goddess of love and daughter of Zeus (Jupiter to the Romans), who walked out of the sea foam at this point as a fully mature woman. She was also known to the Romans as Venus and renowned for her intimate relationships with various gods and mortal men. The site is also along what must be one of the most attractive

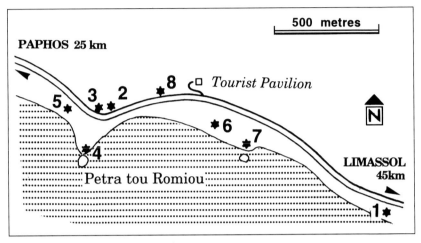

Figure 50: Petra tou Romiou locations.

stretches of coastline in Cyprus with the white chalks and marls of the Upper Lefkara and Pakhna Formations to the east forming spectacular cliffs, rising to nearly 200m. Parking is easy, except during the hottest summer months, and there are eating and toilet facilities, including a Cyprus Tourism Organisation pavilion with splendid views since it is set back above the road. The land hereabouts tend to be unstable due to the plastic and easily eroded nature of some of the clay rocks at beach level, so varying degrees of Recent landslipping can be recognised. This is particularly evident at the well-frequented 'photo-call stop' on the cliff top 1.2km east of Petra tou Romiou (1) (Front cover).

The rocks exposed at Petra tou Romiou are unconformably overlain by the Lefkara Formation chalks and are in the form of an erosional inlier or 'window'. This simply means that we can see them because the overlying chalks have been partly stripped away. They are the easternmost exposures of the late Cretaceous Mamonia Complex (see p. 8), deposited during a relatively short phase, possibly lasting 4 million years, of acute tectonism associated with the convergence and sliding against each other of the African Plate, to the northwest, west and southwest, and the 'Cyprus Microplate' to the southeast, east and northeast. Large and small masses (olistoliths) of disintegrated older igneous and sedimentary rocks, many Triassic, slid into a basin where thick bentonitic clays were being and had been deposited. Some authorities refer to this kind of deposit carrying blocks of mixed composition set in a clay matrix as a melange. The sedimentary and igneous olistoliths found at this locality, all originally displaced from some distant northwesterly source, are known collectively as the Dhiarizos Group.

Despite the immediate attraction of the rock stacks on the beach, it is
advantageous to start investigating this site on the inner core of the main road
above the beach, where it swings round sharply, about 150m west of the ice-
cream kiosk and car park (2). This a fast bend, so take great care with the
constant fast-moving traffic. First you will come across a well-weathered
olistolith of brown lavas and, towards the top of the face, pillows which
characterise lavas poured out into the sea. These lavas have been identified as
Triassic trachytes and trachy-andesites, igneous rocks carrying more silica and
more alkalies than basalts. Sitting directly on the pillow lavas with what appears
to be a normal contact is a small mass of coral-bearing reef limestone also of
Triassic age, and formally part of the Petra tou Romiou Formation. This close
association of what were probably shallow water limestones and lavas is repeated
time and time again in this area, and suggests a palaeogeography in Triassic
times in which there were small volcanic islands or seamounts flanked by reefs.
Another 20m westwards along the roadside (3) then brings you to another block
consisting of a thinly bedded sequence of pink pelagic limestones with chert
layers, again Triassic, but this time probably deposited in deeper waters, away
from the reefs. Resting unconformably on these deposits is a 1m thick pebbly
layer, a residual fragment of one of the late Pleistocene marine terraces or raised
beaches that are strung along this sector of the coastline.

To continue this melange story, now descend to the gravelly beach flanking
the major stacks and examine the largest, which abuts the beach (4). This
consists of hard, brecciated and well-jointed reef limestone in which there is little
semblance of bedding. The angular fragments and the coarsely grained cement
in which they are set have been strongly recrystallised, so that it is difficult to
find fossils. Nonetheless, faint outlines of corals and other reef-living organisms
have been detected which appear to be of Upper Triassic age. There is a narrow
crevice in the centre of the front face, leading up to the top of the stack, and by
glancing up from its foot, or for braver souls ascending it for about 6m, it is
possible to see a well-formed pillow of dark brown trachy-andesitic lava, 60cm
across. This still retains chilled margins produced as the lava came into contact
with sea water. The close association between lavas and reef limestones is again
emphasised.

On the right (western) side of the stack is a remarkable polished face with
parallel grooves sloping at about 45° (Figure 51). This is a slickensided surface.
Slickensides are generated when hard rocks are disrupted, jostled and rubbed
against each other. Such surfaces are produced along faults or by the jostling of
detached masses of well jointed rock during down-slope transport. The latter
origin seems more appropriate here. Many of the blocks outcropping along the
shore show the same feature. If you walk about 150m due west to a large craggy
outcrop (5) running upwards from the back shore to a bench below the road,
you will find a red-brown, recrystallised sandy limestone which is full of such

Figure 51: Slickensided (fine grooved) western face of Triassic reef limestone olistolith.

surfaces. The block shows bedding, though it is difficult to assess the dip because of the very strong jointing. It seems to be steep at about 75° to the southeast.

In back-tracking along the beach past the main stack, and then continuing east along the beach for about 750m, past further limestone olistolith outcrops, note the intermittent outcropping of brown-weathered, non-calcareous bentonitic clay (part of the Kannaviou Formation) (6). This is the matrix material into which the large disoriented rock masses, which you have just been inspecting, slipped, and it would have been in the form of sloppy mud at the time of deposition. It is worthwhile having a look at this material even though it weathers badly and slips easily. In dry weather the surface is a mass of desiccation or shrinkage cracks, which suggests that there are clay minerals within it capable of contraction. In wet weather, in contrast, the clay minerals absorb water, expand and the clay flows more easily. Smectites are prime examples of such clay minerals and they commonly originate from the breakdown of materials, such as pyroxenes or glassy shards of a pumiceous igneous nature. At this locality and inland at Kannaviou (see p. 53) the smectite content is as much as 75%. Understandably, it is these types of contracting and swelling clays which are prone to slip after prolonged wet spells. Other special features of the clays, when *in situ* and fresh, are polished and slickensided fracture surfaces and a fine lamination (foliation). These are best seen in the minor dry stream valleys running northwards off the main road, where the deposits are not affected so much by slipping. The importance of the features is that they indicate that the melange has been subject to considerable tectonic dislocation, such as thrust faulting and overfolding, since its original formation.

Figure 52: Steeply tilted Triassic pillow lavas in olistolith.

Hence, the Mamonia Complex, at least in large part, is a 'tectonised melange'. This contrasts with the Moni 'sedimentary melange', near Limassol (see p. 102) and the Kathikas Melange, north of Paphos (see p. 53), which are only moderately affected by tectonism.

At the end of this traverse across the pebbly beach is a prominent dark headland, with offshore stack (7). The headland is formed mainly of an olistolith of Triassic lavas which are part of the Loudra tis Afroditis Formation (Figure 52). The vesicular rocks, which often have abundant pyroxene and olivine phenocrysts, are potassium-rich basalts, trachy-basalts and, more rarely, andesites. In this respect they differ in chemical detail from the pillow lavas within the Troodos ophiolite. Note the size of some of the bolster-like pillows, as much as 4m wide and 1.75m thick. The more massive lavas show prismatic columnar jointing. The dip of the lavas is steep, 70-80°, almost vertical in places, a disposition indicating that the whole block has been re-orientated considerably during its emplacement. Internal disruption is indicated by polished slickensided surfaces with nearly vertical striations.

Finally, work your way back up the tumbled cliff to the main road by various well-worn paths to the left of the lavas, noting two discrete olistoliths of lava set in the bentonitic matrix. Walk 300m westwards down the main road to where there is an old, narrow metalled road leading off to the north. Here an exposure of *in situ* bentonitic clay matrix can be inspected closely (8).

24. PYRGOS AND PAREKKLISHA (PAREKKLISIA) ROADS

Location. Sheet 24, K717 Series, 1:50,000. 12km east of Limassol, exit northwards from junction 21 on the A1 motorway (Figure 53).

Summary. This itinerary illustrates the essential nature of the late Cretaceous sedimentary Moni Melange and its relationship to adjacent younger Lefkara chalks and older Limassol Forest pillow lavas.

Proceed for a few hundred metres along the Parekklisha road E109 until you reach the F122 road forking off right towards Pyrgos. Park opposite the chalk exposures, taking great care as this is at a fast bend carrying much lorry traffic (1). An outcrop of some 60m of Middle Lefkara Formation creamy white chalks, carrying brown cherts bands and lenticles up to 30cm thick, is distinguished here by the beds being steeply dipping, vertical, overturned, brecciated and generally distorted compared with adjacent Lefkara outcrops to the north and south (Figure 54). By proceeding northwards along the section it soon becomes apparent that the chalks are gradually developing their more regular uniform dip hereabouts of about 50° to the south. What you are looking at is a partial cross-section through the southeasterly extension of the Yerasa Fold and Fault Belt, also seen at Akrounda (Akrounta) about 9km away to the west (see p. 134). It indicates a major phase of tectonic movement in Miocene times when the Limassol Forest ophiolitic mass to the north appears to have been thrust bodily southwards.

Now carry on along the Pyrgos road. The good exposures over the next 2km of ground adjacent to the road tell a fascinating, but rather complicated story. What you will be looking at, in effect, is a typical cross-section through what is known as the Moni Melange or Moni Formation, named after a small village 3.5km to the northeast. This melange is late Cretaceous (Maastrichtian) in age

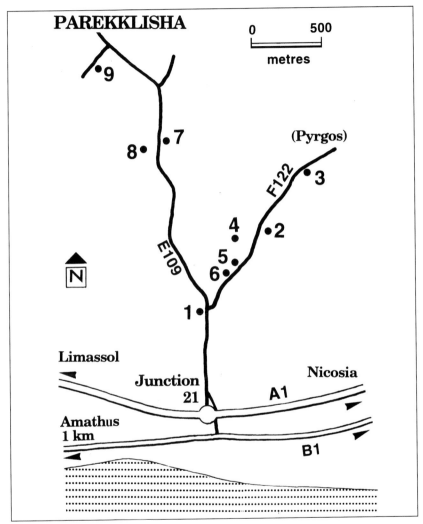

Figure 53: Pyrgos-Parekklisha roads locations.

and the term itself simply means mixture, and that can be readily demonstrated here with a jumble of rocks of mixed lithology and age (Triassic, Jurassic and early Cretaceous) which have been incorporated into a bentonitic clay matrix of late Cretaceous age. The emplacement of these often large bodies of rock (olistoliths) appears to have a consequence of a relatively short-lived episode during late Cretaceous times of gravitational movement of disintegrated older

Figure 54: Steeply dipping Lefkara Formation chalks carrying darker coloured chert layers (C).

Figure 55: Calcrete capping Koronia Member limestones.

rocks, some of shallow water origin, down submarine slopes leading into considerable depths. Some authorities visualise this movement as being in the form of major debris flows. In which case, the Moni Melange can be referred to as a 'sedimentary melange' or 'olistostrome'. The triggering mechanism for these strange events was almost certainly a major phase of collision between adjacent plates in the Cyprus region, one originally to the northwest and west (the African Plate) and one to the southeast and east (the 'Cyprus Microplate').

The two quarries to aim for initially, one large and prominent, the other small and 100m further to the north, occur on the eastern side of the road (2) and comprise some 20m of brown weathering, iron-shot, medium to coarse grained sandstones (156431). These exposures might be united and form one large olistolith or they might be two separate olistoliths. Because of their lithology they are referred to as the Parekklisha Sandstones and are possibly early Cretaceous in age. Jointing within these sandstones is so strong that it is difficult to make out the present true dip of the beds, which seems to be about 20° to the northeast. Not very far away, about 275m along a track running eastwards from the southern end of the main quarry, a prominent outcropping rib of the same sandstone, probably another olistolith, is vertically bedded.

All of these sandstone bodies were clearly jostled about during their emplacement. They appear to have originated from a southerly source, deduced from their angle of repose, but it has to be appreciated that since they were laid down that the whole of the melange has been rotated anticlockwise through 90°. Hence, the source in Cretaceous times really was to the west or even northwest. The ostoliths rest in a clay matrix and this relationship can be partly demonstrated if you walk along the broad ledge at the top of the main quarry, which has a thin capping of weathered bentonitic clay, somewhat mantled by limey downwash. Additionally, by returning to the low cuttings at the roadside opposite the main quarry you can see several small blocks of Parekklisha Sandstone totally enclosed in the clay. Although the clay is weathered to some extent, note that there is little evidence, except immediately in contact with the olistoliths, of polished, slickensided internal surfaces and fine lamination. This indicates that the melange as a whole has been subject to relatively little major internal tectonic deformation subsequent to its emplacement. This is in contrast to parts of the Mamonia Complex, a more tectonised type of melange, near Paphos (see p. 100).

If further proof of the nature of the melange is needed walk northwards along the road for about 500m. In doing so you will see and can inspect on the western side a whole series of sandstone olistoliths outcropping within a short distance from the road. Beneath a prominent and elevated white house with large iron gates on the eastern side of the road a 20m exposure shows a cherty limestone and marl olistolith interdigitating with its clay matrix (3). The limestone is highly jointed and the joint surfaces are often finely grooved and polished, a condition known as slickensiding, which indicates a degree of deformation of the limestone body prior to it coming to its final resting place.

While you have been working these roadside exposures you will have noticed a capping of gently dipping creamy white limestones on both flanks of the valley. These are not olistoliths, but they warrant inspection and are best examined on the western side of the road, immediately opposite the main Parekklisha sandstone quarry. Access is via several old trackways which lead directly towards old, disused limekiln workings (4). The medium grained, well-lithified limestone ribs at the workings (about 7m are exposed) are interbedded with shell-rich marly limestone seams dipping at about 30°

to the northwest, though elsewhere in the same body the dip is much less and to the north. They constitute part of an isolated north-south elongated outcrop of the Koronia Member (Miocene) between the Pyrgos and Parekklisha roads. There are several such Koronia outcrops in this immediate area. The relationship to the underlying melange is one of unconformity and the whole of the older Pakhna and Lefkara Formations, which are normally present in this area beneath the Koronia Member, are missing. This implies that the older sediments were either never deposited on top of the Moni Melange or that they were deposited and then eroded away prior to the deposition of the Koronia Member.

Before you leave this locality note the hardened and somewhat brecciated nature of the uppermost surfaces of the limestones, well seen from the large Parekklisha Sandstone quarry across the valley. This hardening is brought about by weathering processes and secondary calcite cementation, the product being calcrete (Figure 55).

To complete the inspection of this part of the Moni Melange you can either work your way southwards and gently downwards from the limestone workings across scrubby ground for about 170m or you can return down to the road and walk southwards for about the same distance (5). On the west side of the road, and about 30m from it, you will first come across a small disused quarry in a very distinctive green-grey rock, commonly weathered at the top into a ferruginous-looking orange-brown colour. This is serpentinite produced by the hydrothermal alteration of silica-deficient ultrabasic and basic igneous rocks. The rock now consists of highly altered igneous minerals, such as olivines and pyroxenes, which have been converted largely into granular and fibrous serpentine minerals. The prismatic shape of the original minerals can sometimes be detected.

Some 100m south of this quarry there are even more impressive exposures of serpentinite in east-west aligned faces of old workings (6). All these exposures and many more in adjacent fields appear to part of one major arcuate sheet of serpentinite intruded into the melange. This can be mapped intermittently from about 800m east of the quarries to about 1.5km to the northwest. A particularly good quarry occurs on the western side of the Parekklisha road at 146428. It is separated from the Pyrgos road workings on the eastern side by a minor NNW-SSE fault which virtually runs beneath the road at this point.

The origin of these serpentinite sheets is open to some dispute, some authorities suggesting that they are intrusive bodies possibly injected into the melange along contemporary low angle thrust fault or shear planes during or soon after the melange formed. They certainly look brecciated in places and chilled margins have been noted nearby with associated baking of the bentonitic clay. Others think that the sheets may represent serpentinite lavas emitted onto the deep sea floor during the deposition of the melange. Alternatively, the sheets might have slid into place *en bloc* and became embedded in the host muds. What is certain is that the sheets are unrelated in any way to the olistoliths except in occurring within the same melange. The rock types constituting the serpentinites, some resembling altered harzburgite, others looking like altered gabbros, closely resemble rocks occurring within the Troodos and Limassol Forest ophiolites and it seems likely, therefore, that the source was ophiolitic and not too distant.

If you now return to the Parekklisha road and travel northwards for about 1.8km to the southern outskirts of the village, against the football ground (7), there is ample opportunity to examine on the eastern side of the road further olistoliths of Parekklisha Sandstone, which this time carry large secondary concretions of ironstone (limonite) (147437). The exposures commence by the roadside but occur at intervals up the hillside. The dip of the sandstones varies between 25° and 40° to the south and southwest on this side of the hill, but further over the top to the east is as much as 50° eastwards.

By the roadside and a short distance below one of the sandstone outcrops is the first glimpse of the olivine basaltic and basaltic andesite pillow lava succession of the Limassol Forest ophiolite (Campanian). The Moni Melange rests with apparent conformity on the lavas. You are unlikely to see the contact between the two such disparate rock types in a casual visit, but it has been demonstrated that a thin clay separates the sandstones from the lavas, confirming once again that the sandstone bodies are genuine olistoliths.

On the opposite (western) side of the road take the dirt path leading southwestwards down to a marked bluff (8), some 8m high, which consists of pillow breccia, a disintegrated mass of pillow lava and characteristic of the succession hereabouts. The brecciation appears to have been caused by the collapse and disintegration of a pile of pillows, probably at the edge of some depression on the sea floor.

To find typical bulbous pillows, which formed as the lavas poured out on the bottom of the sea, and further pillow breccias you need to move onto the new Parekklisha bypass where, after about 800m, there is a cross-roads with a broad dirt track leading off to the southwest (9) (143445). Parking here is easy and away from the busy main road. The section down the eastern side of the track extends for about 100m and is excellent in demonstrating the close relationship between fresher-looking pillow lavas and the more brown-stained pillow breccias, a relationship brought about in part by faulting. At least two faults can be picked out easily in this section. The brown colour of the breccias is due to a matrix of reddish-brown mudstone.

25. SHA (SIA) COPPER MINE

Location. Sheet 20, K717 Series, 1:50,000. 25km south of Nicosia. Turn off the A1 motorway at junctions 9, 10 or 11 onto the B1, then turn west onto the Sha road at the Mosphiloti cross-roads, where there is a good cafe. Sha mine is 4km from the cross-roads (Figure 43) . Grid reference 342678.

Summary. This old copper mine in the Lower Pillow Lavas is particularly noteworthy for its readily accessible and colourful ochres. A visit to it is worth considering in conjunction with a visit to the Mathiati mine, some 6km away by road, via Mathiatis village. The description of the Mathiati mine also contains additional information about the mineralisation (see p. 87).

The road through Sha village to beyond the mine is metalled, then it changes into a newly widened and much improved dirt road leading towards Mathiatis. The mine is easily recognised through the trees on the south side of the road by the distinctly orange-red spoil heaps flanking it. There are two rutted tracks leading into the pit which is about 100m from the road. Parking is easy on the roadside.

The mine was probably discovered and worked by the ancients, who could hardly miss the signs of the presence of such resources with all the red and orange colours of ochre in the surface soils, but the extent and thickness of the

Figure 56: Red and yellow ochres (O) to the right of the face overlain by unaffected Upper Pillow Lava (P).

relatively small orebody, which consisted of two lenses located at the top of the Lower Pillow Lavas were only confirmed by drilling in 1929. Work ceased in the 1970's. The amount of ore present totalled about 500,000 tons. The dominant ore mineral is pyrites (iron sulphide), but silvery marcasite (another iron sulphide) is also prominent and currently seems easier to find in the workings. Copper pyrites (chalcopyrites) is present in small amounts, the copper percentage varying between 0.25-1.20 per cent.

On entering the partially flooded pit at its northern end, the first features of interest can be clearly seen on the uppermost bench leading off to the left. What looks like a channel in cross-section is in fact the irregular base of a brown-weathered basaltic lava sheet belonging to the Upper Pillow Lavas. It rests directly on a multi-hued pocket of soft friable ochre, a material formed predominantly of varying concentrations of hydrated iron oxides and still used as a pigment (Figure 56). The ochre has yielded small amounts of gold and silver. It is the ochre which colours the spoil heaps. Cyprus ochres usually rest directly on top of the metallic ore bodies and were created by submarine weathering, in this instance before the eruption of the Upper Pillow Lavas (see Back Cover, bottom).

Return to the sloping track leading down the eastern side of the pit, the faces of which are obscured somewhat by downwash and rock falls. Recent secondary gypsum is widespread underfoot and is a mineral which forms quite quickly during the chemical decay and oxidation of any residual sulphide minerals in the spoil. The flooded area is the site of the once worked highly brecciated stockwork zone beneath the original massive ore bodies. Through this stockwork the hot mineralising fluids invaded the Lower Lavas, impregnating them with sulphides. By looking at the concentrations of dark-looking fallen blocks you will be able to pick out the position of a number of near vertical, altered doleritic dykes, up to 2m thick, cutting through the mineralised and highly altered Lower Lavas. These dykes acted as feeders for the Upper Lavas. They also post-date the ore and ochre so are not mineralised. The southern end of the accessible part of the pit is usually the most productive for mineral specimens, especially in loose blocks.

26. SKOURIOTISSA COPPER MINE

Location. Sheet 10, K717 Series, 1;50,000. About 45km due west of Nicosia on the B9 as far as the T-junction with the E908 Linou and Kalapanayiotis road. 3km from the junction turn right (northwards) onto a minor metalled road leading through Katydhata (Figure 57). Grid reference 907840.

Note: You are very close to the U.N. controlled demarkation line, which runs just to the north of the spoil heaps, so exert great discretion in what you do. Keep to the designated itinerary.

Summary. Skouriotissa, 'Our Lady of the Slag Heaps', is the doyen of all the copper-bearing ore bodies of Cyprus, one of the largest and longest-lived. It occurs in the Pillow Lava sequence of the Troodos ophiolite.

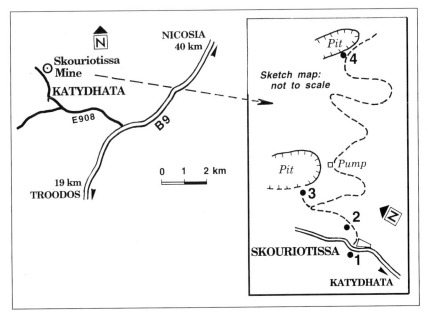

Figure 57: Skouriotissa mine locations.

Skouriotissa is by far the most historically interesting copper mine on the island. Over the centuries it has become progressively exhausted and, by the 1970's, with world copper prices at a low, any major activity at it had virtually ceased. In the 3rd millennium B.C. the deposits were being worked for jewellery, crucibles and implements. Charcoal fragments associated with some of the slag has been radiocarbon dated as 2760 B.C. The Mycenaeans and Phoenicians developed the industry, but probably the greatest expansion occurred during Roman times from 30 B.C. to A.D 330, by surface working and by extensive underground galleries and shafts. Between them the ancients probably removed two and half million tons of ore. The Mycenaean smelters used manganese as a flux, possibly derived from local outcrops of umber, and it has turned their slags to brown and reddish-brown, whereas the Roman slags are black. In the Middle Ages mining activity diminished considerably, only to be revived during the 1920's and early 1930's. The youngest waste material is multicoloured due to the displacement of large amounts of ochre, which capped the original ore bodies. By the 1970's about another four hundred million tons of ore had been removed.

The vast spoil and slag heaps, somewhat obscuring the solid geology for the casual visitor, contain more than half of that produced by the mines in Cyprus, and come into view while on the A9 road. So, there is no real problem in finding your way and eventually finding a good parking place at their foot, adjacent to the site of the old mine camp on the east side of the road (1).

Figure 58: Roman slag heaps, with Troodos Range in the background.

Skouriotissa is essentially two ore bodies, the most westerly adjacent to the road is known as the Phoenix mine and 1km to the east is the Skouriotissa Mine proper. A major north-south trending fault, with a downthrow on its eastern side separates the two. The whole area is characterised by major faults, many oriented roughly north-south, some post-dating the mineralisation, others pre-dating it. The latter created rift-valley (graben) depressions on the surface of the Pillow Lavas, the one encompassing this mine and others nearby being known as the Solea Graben. Suggestions have been put forward that many of these older faults acted as feeders for the mineralising gaseous fluids (re-circulated and heated sea water) which emanated from several kilometres depth. The ores were laid down as chemical precipitates on the irregular upper surface of the lavas in the form of thin lenses of restricted size.

Take the well defined access track leading off from the camp site towards the upstanding masses of black Roman slag (2) (Figure 58). Continue up the track beyond the next U-bend until you come to a flattish bench overlooking the large multicoloured and flat bottomed Phoenix Pit (3) (Figure 9). (On no account must you stray near to the lip of this or any other pit at this locality or try to descend the unstable and dangerous faces which are very prone to slipping. The bottoms of the pits are quagmires and are partly flooded with toxic chemicals).

This is the site of the ore body which appears to have been a stockwork penetrating through the Lower Pillow Lavas and into the Upper Pillow Lavas. Some authorities believe that this structure was located beneath and acted as a feeder for the original Skouriotissa massive ore body, which rested on the upper surface of the Upper Pillow Lavas. The theory being that the Skouriotissa ore body was subsequently separated from the Phoenix feeder either by faulting or by some kind of sea-bottom gravity sliding. An alternative view is that there were two totally separate ore bodies, the Phoenix either not developing a massive ore at its top or losing the massive top to subsequent erosion soon after it was formed. There is some evidence for a stockwork beneath the Skouriotissa main body, which originally had a flat-lying lens shape measuring 671m long, 213m wide and with a maximum thickness of 150m.

Figure 59: Phoenix mine.

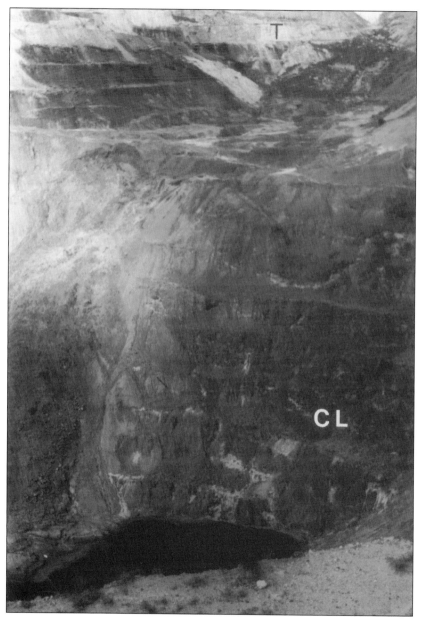

Figure 60: Skouriotissa mine with Tertiary limestone capping (T). Chloritised lavas (CL).

The metallic sulphide content of the ore mined from the pits was relatively simple with abundant primary pyrites admixed with minor amounts of primary copper pyrites (chalcopyrites) and traces of the precious metals gold and silver. There was a range of secondary copper minerals due to secondary leaching by sea-water, such as chalcocite, which is another copper sulphide. The overall copper content in the massive ore was of the order of 2.5 per cent, diminishing in the stockworks to percentages as low as 0.9 per cent.

From the bench of this first, most westerly pit, the most striking visible features from left to right, as you look towards the northeast and east, are faces of iron-stained chocolate-brown lavas passing laterally into highly altered green chloritised lavas which carry sulphide veins. The alteration by hot hydrothermal fluids occurred during the mineralisation. This is in contrast to the capping of multicoloured ochreous material above the lavas, not all of which is strictly *in situ*. Ochres are produced by cold water submarine weathering and leaching of ore bodies. At these mines the ochres form a thick deposit composed mainly of brown, yellow and red iron oxides, with a sprinkling of sulphides derived from the ore, together with secondary chert. One of the distinctive features of the ochres is that they show evidence of re-working by the sea bottom currents, with features such as bedding, lamination and graded bedding. Some of the ochres were transported away from their point of origin by natural sea bottom processes and now appear to rest directly on non-mineralised lavas.

Return to the U-turn and take the relatively steeply inclined track leading upwards and eastwards. After about 250m you again U-turn roughly northwards and head towards a derelict pumping station situated on a north-facing edge of the spoil heaps. As you work your way upwards there is ample opportunity to examine loose material at the side of the track for good mineral specimens. Excellent euhedral crystals of pyrites can be found in cubes up to 1.5 cm in size and showing typical striated faces. In many specimens you can pick up, the pyrites aggregates are associated with smaller crystals of brassy-yellow copper pyrites and black grains of chalcocite. All these ore minerals are frequently set in an orange-brown matrix containing quartz and gypsum grains.

The zig-zag route involving four more U-turns now takes you up various inclined tracks towards the top of the spoil heaps, initially overlooking the Phoenix pit. The basic principle to adopt in route-finding is to keep ascending with the pits as closeby as possible on your left hand side, so that you are nearly always overlooking them. A few hundred metres of rising track takes you to the site of the pump, which was part of the mining plant and used for extracting copper by leaching processes. (You could not approach the plant if it was working, because of the acid water which tended to spray from the machinery). Soon you will see the deep and impressive, partially flooded pit, which is the Skouriotissa Mine proper (4) (Figure 60). By standing carefully on the grassy ledge above the southern edge of the pit you will observe a terraced outcrop of brown Upper Pillow Lavas on the right, and these are very clearly faulted against the green, chloritised mineral zone associated with the now worked-out main ore body. Extraction of ore eventually extended into what appears to have been a stockwork zone, originally located beneath the chloritised alteration zone. Ochreous weathering of the orebody is again evident in the orange, brown and red patches you can see towards the top of the pit. A certain degree of slipping has affected this material.

If you look across to the higher parts of the pit and adjacent ridge you might be able to pick out patches of chocolate brown umber of the late Cretaceous (Campanian) Parapedhi Formation resting on the Upper Pillow Lavas. The light coloured limestones capping the ridge belong to the younger Pakhna Formation and Koronia Member. These rocks are accessible if you can find your way around the top of the Skouriotissa Pit, but it is preferable and safer to examine these rocks elsewhere (Margi for umbers, p. 80).

During the ascent on a clear day you will see increasingly splendid views of Morphou Bay and the northwestern end of the main Troodos ophiolite range. The low-lying ground adjacent to the bay and running eastwards is an extension of the Mesaoria Plain, and is essentially mantled by Quaternary deposits. By casting your eyes westwards towards the distant peak and headland you can see the jetty just to the west of Karavostasi (meaning 'safe anchorage for sailing vessels'), where a major ore crushing plant operated into the 1970's, servicing both the Skouriotissa mine and the Mavrovouni Mine, located 5km away to the west and now inaccessible. From Mavrovouni, a much larger sulphide stockwork than at the Skouriotissa mines, some 15 million tons of ore have been extracted.

27. STAVROVOUNI ROAD

Location. Sheet 20, K717 Series, 1:50,000. 6km south-southeast of junction 11 A1 road. Access is via the B1 road and the road sign at the Stavrovouni T-junction reads Limassol 47km, Nicosia 29km (Figure 61).

Summary. Excellent exposures in the Sheeted Dyke Complex (the Diabase Group) of the main Troodos ophiolite, plus a magnificent viewpoint looking into ophiolite country and at the circum-ophiolite sedimentary succession.

Stavrovouni (Mountain of the Cross) is a very prominent 688m high pinnacle of rock at the eastern extremity of the main Troodos ophiolite mass. On its peak is the site of Cyprus's oldest monastery founded by Helena, the mother of Constantine the Great, in A.D. 327. Since then it has been burnt down and was only rebuilt in the last century. It operates a strict all-male regime and women are not allowed to enter at any time.

The metalled access road to Stavrovouni passes working quarries (382626) on the northern side of the road in the basic igneous Basal Group, the lowest

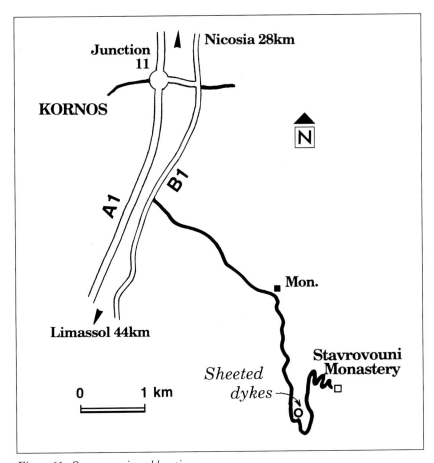

Figure 61: Stavrovouni road locations.

member of the Pillow Lava succession in the ophiolite complex, but access is difficult. Continue southeastwards along the rising road past the army camp and Ayia Varvara (Saint Barbara) monastery for about 1.7km until you reach a col with splendid views opening out to the south (393602). From the ample parking space, adjacent to a road sign, there is a galaxy of radiating dirt tracks cut along the terraced slopes, which can form the basis of gentle country walks.

From the col the metalled road to the top now swings through a series of sharp curves, indicated by Z-bend notices, exposing for the next 200m excellent sections through the Sheeted Dyke Complex (Diabase Group) level within the Troodos ophiolite (see p. 10). The best face to examine is the first east-west one you come across on the left hand side and is about 50m long (Figure 62). The section exhibits a high proportion of dykes separated by basic igneous rock screens, the original *in situ* country rock. The dykes dip eastwards at angles varying between 65-80° and with an approximate north-south orientation. They vary in thickness, some approaching 2m, and are coloured orange-brown and green-grey, the colour reflecting the differential weathering of rocks of slightly variable mineral composition. Essentially the dykes were mainly basic doleritic bodies when emplaced, but at some early stage in their subsequent history they were altered, by hydrothermal metamorphic reaction with invasive sea water, into diabases. Diabases contain albite plagioclase feldspar, green chlorite and epidote as a consequence of these changes.

Figure 62: Sheeted dykes.

The features of greatest interest, however, are found at the margins of the dykes and are referred to as chilled margins. Particularly clear examples occur here (Figure 63). A chilled margin is marked by a very fine grained, almost glassy-looking dark coloured zone, usually less than a centimetre in thickness, formed by rapid cooling at the margins of a hot igneous body when it is intruded into and against a pre-existing colder rock. The relatively fast cooling prevents the formation of large crystals at the margins of the intrusion whereas the inner, more slowly cooling part of the body, does allow it.

Figure 63: Chilled dyke margin (the dark edge (C) to the left of the cm scale bar).

A considerable amount of research has been done on the Troodos Dyke Complex in Cyprus and it has been estimated that dyke intrusion, by the infilling of tension fractures, must have brought about a crustal extension of between 100-120km. Sea-floor spreading is the only suitable mechanism which could bring about this extension. Multiple or sheeted dykes are known to be usually orientated parallel to spreading axes, and many of the dykes in this complex are at present orientated roughly north-south and northwest-southeast. Hence, allowing for faulting and tilting subsequent to their intrusion, it could be deduced that they paralleled spreading axes with a similar orientation at the time of formation of the ophiolite. But what complicates the story is that geomagnetic work on these dykes has demonstrated that they have been rotated anticlockwise as a whole through 90° since they were intruded. So, initially, in late Cretaceous times, the spreading axes were really orientated approximately east-west to northeast-southwest.

From this locality it is now very worthwhile ascending to the top of Stavrovouni, where there are adequate parking and toilet facilities, to inspect the magnificent all-round view. Note the red ochreous breccias and chloritised patches in the Dyke Complex on the way up. The monastery is built on the Complex, flanked by the Basal Group, and on the footslopes to the east of the peak the passage upwards into Pillow Lavas, with smoother, lower-lying topography, purple-brown outcrops and soils can be readily observed. But the rocks which are most prominent, and sweep round in a large arc from south to north, are the creamy white chalk escarpments of the Lefkara Formation that form the sedimentary cover of the ophiolites. On a clear day, towards the south and east, the low-lying Quaternary coastal zone with Larnaca Airport and adjacent salt lakes can just be picked out. To the northeast, about 23km distant, is the prominent hump-backed hill, known as the Troulli inlier. This is the most easterly outcrop of the Troodos ophiolite, formed mainly of pillow lavas, and is now totally isolated from the main outcrop by younger sedimentary rocks. The view to the north encompasses Nicosia and the Kyrenia Range in the far distance and in the foreground the extensive quarries in the Basal Group at the foot of the lead-in road. Looking westwards into the rugged heart of the Troodos Mountains the view is splendid, especially at low angles of the sun.

28. TOKHNI (TOCHNI)

Location. Sheet 20, K717 Series, 1:50,000. 5km to the northeast of exit 15 on the A1 Limassol-Nicosia motorway (Figure 64). Grid reference 296490.

Summary. This locality is very good for relatively shallow water sedimentary features, including channel-fill conglomerates, sheet flow and bioturbation structures, within the Miocene Pakhna Formation, the shelly reef facies of the overlying Koronia Formation, also convoluted structures within the Kalavasos Formation salt deposits.

Tokhni is a village being developed as a holiday home centre and is situated at the entrance of a narrow NNW-SSE fault-controlled gorge. At its heart is a well-maintained small, but prominent, church with toilet facilities nearby. The roads are narrow, though parking for cars is no real problem. Coaches need to stop some 200m short of the church.

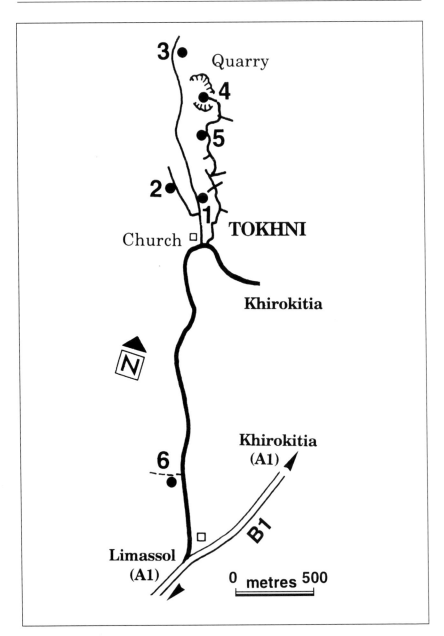

Figure 64: Tokhni locations.

Fifty metres NNW beyond the church the metalled road changes into a dirt track running along the eastern side of the gorge. It is worthwhile examining the beds on both side of the gorge for the next 500m or so and there are several cross-paths and tracks which readily allow this. Take care when approaching the foot of the cliffs as they are prone to rock falls.

Immediately on the right hand side of the lead-in track behind a few citrus trees is a low cliff which exposes coarse conglomerates (1). A little further on, with the vertical cliff faces more prominent, look across to the western side and note towards the top of the lower cliffs the same conglomeratic body, dipping towards the south-southeast. It contains large boulders of creamy chalky limestone, anything up to a metre in size. A particularly striking feature is the sharp basal contact, with the conglomerate cutting down into the underlying beds. The relationship of this conglomerate to the adjacent beds is not as obvious as it might appear. Some authorities consider it to be simply a coarser layer laid down during an episode of powerful submarine current activity towards the end of Pakhna times. By viewing the whole series of outcrops leading up the sides of the gorge, this interpretation seems quite valid. On the other hand, it might be that the conglomerate is younger in age than the adjacent rocks, possibly Pliocene or Pleistocene, and deposited from powerful subaerial streams along the line of pre-existing valleys during periods of high rainfall. What do you think ?

The bulk of the Pakhna Formation rocks forming the sides of the gorge near the village are massively bedded, brown, calcareous sandstones and sandy limestones, with individual beds up to 1.2m thick, interbedded with thinner flags. Their dip is low, about 20° to the south-southeast. The beds have been quarried in the past, so that part of the gorge is man-made. Quarrying is still taking place further up, as indicated by the fresh spoil heaps. The individual constituents of the beds are difficult to identify in hand-specimen, but include grains of quartz, feldspar, chert and pyroxenes. The pyroxene is a variety known as diopside, the source of which is likely to have been the ophiolite pillow lavas, now exposed to the north, which are rich in that ferro-magnesian silicate. Other components are detrital calcite grains and broken fragments of marine organisms, such as foraminifera, bryozoa and algae. Casts of gastropods and brachiopods are present at certain levels, but recrystallisation and secondary cementation makes identification very difficult. At the tops of some of the massive beds and within the flags, standing-out well because of colour differences, occur a variety of horizontal and oblique tubes (trace fossils) up to a centimetre across. These witness the activities of burrowing organisms during quieter periods of deposition.

Perhaps the most striking feature of some of the massive beds is the presence of pebbles, boulders and flat slabs (rafts) of creamy chalk within them, which have been identified as coming from the immediately underlying Lefkara

Formation (Late Cretaceous-Oligocene) (2) (Figure 65). Their presence in the Pakhna indicates that they must have been well lithified before being subject to erosion and transportation. Precisely how they were transported is conjectural, but it is commonly believed that they were picked-up and 'floated' within highly mobile bottom-hugging sheets of sediment moving down gentle slopes on the sea floor. This process is known as sheet flow. (See Yermasoyia Road, p. 133).

Figure 65: 'Rafted' Lefkara Formation chalk fragments (boulders and pebbles) in darker Pakhna Formation sediments.

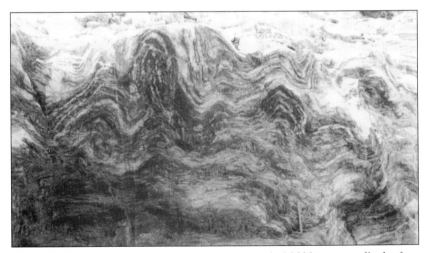

Figure 66: Contorted gypsum beds. The uppermost vertical fold has an amplitude of about 35cm.

Proceed along the right hand track, keeping below the foot of the spoil heaps caused by the dumping of waste from the hill top quarry. Emerging out of the waste material, on the right hand side, are intermittent outcrops of the strongly jointed and fractured creamy white marly chalks of the Lefkara Formation (3). Some of the exposures look like slipped blocks, relationships being difficult to determine, but there is no doubt that the junction between the Pakhna and underlying Lefkara Formations is nearby. The lithology of the older rocks is quite distinct and is formed practically entirely of fine grained calcite in which minute spheres can be seen with a hand lens, these being microfossils known as foraminifera. These deposits are envisaged as having been laid down as a calcareous ooze in clearer seas and at greater depths than for the local Pakhna Formation.

Now walk up the rough track into the actively working quarry perched on the lip of the gorge (4) (295495). In the piles of sawn and broken flaggy slabs, commonly used for facing purposes, are good examples of bioturbation of the original soft sediment by the surface grazing and burrowing activities of soft-bodied organisms. Ripple marked faces also occur. Note the well-developed joint planes in the bottom of the quarry and in the vertical quarry faces. These are a witness to late Miocene fold and fault movements in the region.

The route then takes you out of the quarry on its eastern side and loops round southwards for about 200m towards the village, along well-defined dirt tracks between cultivated fields. The objective is in sight from the quarry exit and is a prominent upstanding craggy knoll (5) (296494). If you approach directly from the village *en route* to the quarry, the knoll is on the left of the pathway. The hard blocks are light grey limestones belonging to the Miocene Koronia Limestone Formation. They are devoid of bedding and are full of small cavities (vughs), the latter indicative of the original structure of the limestones and solution effects during subsequent weathering. Despite the rock having been subject to these processes and recrystallisation it is still possible to detect the moulds and casts of a range of fossils, such as bivalves, bryozoa and rare corals. Laminated algal structures, commonly spherical, are also present and it is these features, combined with the overall lithological character of the beds, which imply that the formation at this locality belongs to a 'reef facies'. Facies is a technical term referring to the characteristics of a rock unit which reflect specific environmental conditions. The algal reefs were probably not of large dimensions in height or lateral extent and appear to have developed in a patchy fashion on a shallow water shelf-like area fringing the southeastern flanks of an emerging 'Troodos land mass'.

The path back to the village runs essentially southwards, with the water tank to the right (west) initially, then a passage between some buildings towards the built-up area. A number of zig-zag downhill passage-ways brings you back onto the main road adjacent to the church.

The next locality is 1.75km south of Tokhni village, some 300m from the old main Nicosia road (6) (294472). It comprises two north-facing shallow quarries on the west side of the Tokhni road, rising towards the west. Within these old workings are exposed at least 5m of gypsum beds, assigned to the Miocene Kalavasos Formation. The boundary between this formation and the Koronia Formation, seen at the last locality, is one of interdigitation and it is likely that at least some of the gysum deposits were laid down in shallow lagoons protected from the sea by reefs (see Maroni, p. 83).

Gypsum is widespread in this area and the mineral takes on many forms (see Kalavasos, p. 51). Some beds are sugary, coarse to medium grained in texture and within these there are individual grains, pockets and lenses of secondary transparent selenite, commonly showing swallow-tail twinning structure. Some crystalline gypsum is in the form of secondary nodules, which distort or destroy the original bedding. Thin layers of very fine grained, light brown to white alabaster are present. Other beds, referred to as 'marmara' in Cyprus, and used as paving flags and tiles, are markedly laminated. The laminated beds in the top 2m of the southernmost quarry exhibit internal buckling and contortion, the origin of which is open to debate (Figure 66) (see Kalavasos, p. 51). Some believe it is caused by the conversion of primary anhydrite (a non-hydrated form of calcium sulphate) into its hydrated equivalent gypsum, a change which involves a volume increase. Others favour post-depositional slumping of plastic beds down shallow slopes on the sea floor. Note that the layers above the contorted level are unaffected; this is good evidence in favour of early post-depositional displacement. The direction of movement can sometimes be inferred from the orientation of the fold axes, especially if they are overturned, the assumption being that the 'noses' of the folds point down the original sea bottom slope. At this locality the evidence is not too clear, as the axes of many of the folds are near-vertical, but there are a few which suggest that the slope might have been to the southeast. If slumping is a valid explanation for these structures, then a triggering mechanism could have been earth tremors mobilising the soft sediment on the sea floor during Kalavasos times. As this particular slumped layer can be traced for some 5km, there seems to be some justification for an earthquake hypothesis. The reason for the earthquake could have been movement along a fault located in the underlying ophiolitic basement.

29. TROODOS (TROODHOS)

Location. Sheet 18, K717 Series, 1:50,000. Troodos, though not really a village, but which has eating establishments, open air stalls and toilet facilities, is the focal point located at grid reference 890649. It is 78km from Nicosia along the B9 road and about 55km from Limassol via the B8 road. These two roads bisecting the Troodos Range are of excellent quality, as is the E801 connecting the B8 at Trimiklini with the B9 to the north. All other connecting roads are narrow in places, often single-tracked and can be poorly surfaced (Figure 67).

Summary. This tour illustrates some of the plutonic core rocks of the Troodos ophiolite.

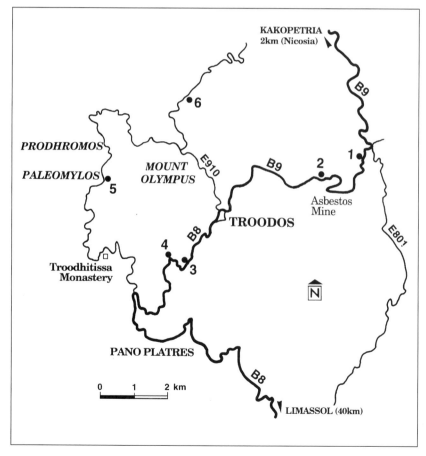

Figure 67: Troodos locations.

The Troodos Mountains are said to be the most magical part of the island with excellent views from Mount Olympus (1952m) and other roadside vantage points, stretching from the Kyrenia Range and Morphou Bay in the north to Paphos, Limassol and Larnaca in the south. Deeply entrenched valleys and narrow spurs, around which the roads gyrate and cling precariously, are shaded by mixed woodland in which cedars, pines and oaks are prominent. Cedar Valley, 18km due northwest of Troodos village, is a noted beauty spot with one cedar reaching a height of 30m and estimated as having germinated about 850 years ago. Snow persists in the summit area until April, and during winter blocks some of the minor side roads. Rock falls from the innumerable outcrops can be a driving hazard at these times. No visit to the Troodos Range should omit looking around some of the Byzantine monasteries and churches. Troodhitissa, the highest working monastery in the land, is one such, located on a prime southeast-facing sunny slope accessed from a minor winding road to the south of Mount Olympus. It was first founded in 1250, but rebuilt twice after forest fires, lastly in 1731.

Mount Olympus, with its radar globes and radio masts, and Troodos lie at the heart of the late Cretaceous (Campanian) ophiolite complex, a mass of oceanic lithosphere, some 11-20km thick, now detached by thrust faulting (obduction), rotated though 90° anticlockwise and uplifted after having originated at a spreading ridge on the sea bottom. The shape of the mass is consistent with its emplacement on continental crust by thrusting. The elevation into an elongated dome occurred mainly during late Miocene to Pleistocene times. The plutonic core of complex comprises medium to coarse grained basic and ultrabasic igneous rocks, many of which seem to have been intruded from multiple magma chambers distributed at varying depths along several fault-bounded spreading axes. In this area the rocks are strongly faulted and interdigitate with each other in a very complicated fashion. Both field recognition of the rock types, many of which have undergone subsequent alteration, and precise outcrop location using tourist maps, creates problems for the casual visitor. So, a degree of persistence and 'jumping in and out of vehicles' is required to get to some grips with the story. All the rock names mentioned below are defined in the Glossary.

Two major plutonic sequences of rocks can be recognised, each derived from different magma sources. The earlier sequence consists of tectonised hartzburgite, believed to have been derived from the upper levels of the Earth's mantle, dunite carrying chrome minerals, pyroxenite and gabbro, all often showing evidence of high-temperature internal deformation. Vertical banding (foliation to geologists) trending roughly northwest – southeast in these rocks, and caused by the alignment of pyroxene, spinel and olivine grains, shows marked discordance with the physical boundaries of the rock units. It is taken to indicate upwards and lateral movement of the various plastic igneous magmas during spreading activity.

The later sequence, possibly derived from isolated magma chambers distributed throughout the earlier sequence, intrudes (cross-cuts) into the earlier as undeformed masses and consists of peridotites, pyroxenites and gabbros, with diorites and plagiogranites at higher levels. To complicate matters even further the harzburgites and dunites, since emplacement, have been subject to hydrothermal alteration by invasive sea water converting them into low density serpentinites, and these secondary products, highly mobile in character, have intruded adjacent rocks. It has been claimed that the upwards displacement of the serpentinite bodies by gravitational forces accounts in part for the intermittent elevation of the Troodos Range from late Cretaceous times onwards, though more especially during Miocene and Pleistocene times. Taking into account the thickness of the ophiolite, the depth of the sea during Cretaceous times and the present elevation of the Range, the total vertical elevation could amount to 15km or more.

The first locality (1) is about 500m westwards from the major road junction of the B9 Nicosia-Troodos road, the E801 leading upwards from the south (933665) and the E909 Khandria road from the east. On the west side of the road is a re-entrant in the cliffs floored by a small coppice. The cliffs are predominantly formed of gabbros. But what is distinctive about the right hand face is the presence of a dolerite (diabase) dyke and, more especially, a number of light coloured vein-like intrusions of plagiogranite (an albite feldspar, quartz, amphibole rock) all leading up the face. The plagiogranite veins are up to 10cm wide in places and are relatively highly siliceous in composition compared with the gabbros, suggesting that they separated out in a basic magma chamber at depth at some late stage in the evolution of the plutonic sequence of rocks. Epidote, a yellowish-green mineral is present. Try and work out whether the basic dyke intrusion post-dated the plagiogranite veins, as is commonly the case elsewhere on Troodos.

Undoubtedly, the next locality (2) is the easiest to find on Troodos (Figure 68). It is the impressive, but unsightly, asbestos opencast mine at Pano Amiandos, about 4.5 km east of Troodos, adjacent to the main access road from Nicosia (924656). Amanthius, meaning undefiled, is the name ancients gave to asbestos, an allusion to the fact that cloth woven from it cleaned easily when thrown into a fire. The mine began to be actively exploited in 1904 and is one of the largest in Europe, but has ceased working consequent on the world-wide recognition of asbestos-related health problems. At its peak several million tonnes of ore were processed annually from which were concentrated 20 to 40 thousand tonnes of asbestos (chrysotile) fibre. Chrysotile is one of the commercial varieties of asbestos and is a white to greenish fibrous serpentine mineral. The chrysotile fibres are up to 1.5cm long and occur in veins up to

1.5cm thick cutting through fault-brecciated serpentinitised harzburgite rock. They are associated with white picrolite, another low temperature serpentine mineral. Although there are several good viewpoints, one of the best is a kilometre beyond the very sharp U-bend and at a higher altitude (921658). There, on the top road, you not only get a better impression of the scale of the workings but you can also inspect the worked rock *in situ*, shot through with cross-fibred veins of asbestos.

Figure 68: Overview of Amiandos asbestos mine.

From here to Troodos village there are many outcrops of serpentinised harzburgite with well-developed foliation defined by the orientation of pyroxenes, which form about 20 per cent of the rock. The rest of the rock is composed of serpentinised olivine.

From the village centre travel southwestwards for 2.5km down the B8 Pano Platres road. Rhythmically layered gabbros belonging to the early suite of rocks are excellently exposed for about 100m on the west side of the road (3) (878632). There is a blue signpost at the top end of the section indicating Troodos and Residencies, and there is a perched green bungalow at the bottom end. The outcrops are separated from the road side by a gentle and narrow downwash slope, which can be scrambled up with no difficulty. The apparent dip of about 20° to the south of the relatively continuous layers parallels the slope of the road surface. The layers are 1-40cm thick and are made distinct by their variations in colour, green-grey, brown and cream, due to differing proportions of light and dark minerals (Figure 69). Close inspection shows that

Figure 69: Layered gabbros. Scale in centimetres.

certain of the layers show pseudo-sedimentary structures, including vertical grading from coarse bases to finer grained tops, sharp, almost scoured, basal contacts, cross-lamination and slump structures. These features indicate a certain degree of gravitational settlement within the intrusive magma chamber plus plastic flow. The occurrence of plastic flow is substantiated by the strongly preferred orientation of the olivines, pyroxenes and plagioclase feldspars parallel to the layering. Note that the gabbros have been intruded by two cross-cutting igneous bodies, up to 2m thick, and which appear to have affinities with harzburgite.

Continue down the Pano Platres road for about 1km until you see a loop of the original, now disused road on the right (4) (872634). Park at the roadside, then walk along the remains of the old road towards a narrow bridge, built in 1930. The bridge is against a small waterfall and solitary pine tree. Before you get to the bridge is an excellent 8m high section showing the junction between mantle-derived harzburgite and crustal dunite – the 'Petrologic Moho'. The grey-green harzburgite shows marked foliation, defined by the orientation of pyroxenes and dark chrome spinels (chromium-bearing magnesium aluminium oxides). The contact with the deeply orange-weathered dunite (an olivine-dominated rock) is very obvious about 29m from the bridge and, in contrast with many such contacts in the Troodos plutonic core is concordant with the foliation in the harzburgite.

Continue down the twisting B8 road for about another 3km then at a sharp U-bend take a right fork onto a narrow road leading to the Post-Byzantine Troodhitissa Monastery, which is well worth a visit (5). There are precipitous slopes on the left hand side of the road with splendid views southwards.

About 5km beyond the monastery you will eventually come across a small stream running westwards towards Paleomylos (6) (853657). The road does a right angled turn to the left at this point and about 20m beyond the turn, on the right hand side of the road, is an outcrop of very coarse grained pyroxenite, with individual lustrous grains reaching a size of 20-30 cm. **On no account must this exposure be hammered**. What you are looking at is a pegmatitic lens, one of several, emplaced in wehrlite, and created by very hot gaseous fluids invading the wehrlite and cooling sufficiently slowly to allow the formation of these abnormally large sized pyroxenes.

Continue northwards to Prodhromos and turn right onto the Troodos road (F952) and follow it until you are about 250m north of the bottom of a Ski Lift (876667). Directly opposite a stone building and Nature Trail notice is a poor quality dirt track leading downwards and essentially northwards, skirting a number of old buildings. The track is barely suitable for 4-wheel drive vehicles and the walking distance of about 2km to some derelict chrome mine buildings (6) (878683) takes about 30 minutes each way. For most of the way you are, in effect, travelling near to a north-south trending vertical contact between harzburgites and brown-weathered dunites, and it is in the much faulted transition zone between the two, about 50m wide, that the chromite (chrome iron oxide) occurs. In the immediate vicinity of the chrome mine and nearby drained ponds (beyond which the track deteriorates) loose fragments and *in-situ* segregated lenses and pods of the iron-black to brownish-black chromite, enclosed in dunite, can be found. They are small in size and you need to be rather an expert chromitologist to detect them. The bulk of the workings were underground at depths up to 400m. Between the 1920's and 1970's, when mining ceased, something of the order of 600,000 tons of ore were extracted. Chromite grains are a primary mineral present in most ultrabasic and many basic rocks, but need to be concentrated, as here, by natural segregation processes in fluid magma before reaching the status of an economic ore. Even then the chromite has to be separated from the country rock before becoming commercially viable. This work was carried out some 5km further down the valley and brought about a 47 per cent chromite concentration.

From this location the track is so poor that it is better to return back to the main road leading to Troodos village.

30. YERMASOYIA (GERMASOGEIA) ROAD

Location. Sheet 23, K717 Series, 1:50,000. Junction 24 on the A1 northwards for 6km as far as Akrounda (Akrounta) (Figure 70).

Summary. This south to north itinerary consists of a number of irregularly spaced, but readily accessible locations along the F128 roadside in which the local geological succession can be seen descending from the shelly Middle Miocene Pakhna Formation at the southern end, via the Oligocene to Eocene Lefkara Formation, to the late Cretaceous Moni Melange at the northern end.

Note. This itinerary can be extended to include the circular tour of Limassol Forest (see p. 72).

The first stop (1) is on the west side of the road some 250m from the A1 roundabout where there is a virtually continuous exposure of the Pakhna Formation (080410). The strata dip gently southwards at 6°-20°. The rocks are light brown, rather coarse grained, shelly sandy limestones and marls in rapidly alternating layers varying in thickness from 1.5m to centimetre scale. If you work your way slowly along the foot of the exposures as far as the water fountain a wealth of interesting sedimentary details will begin to emerge. These include scour channels-with very sharp discordant bases, which cut down as much as 1m into the underlying layers. One such is about 8m south of the Football Ground signpost and measures at least 2.5m across. The channel fill is of breccia formed of angular Pakhna fragments, some contorted, intermingled with rather lighter creamy white fragments, up to 50cm across, of older Lefkara Formation age. Sharp basal contacts caused by scour are common at the base of many of the light brown layers and this gives some indication of the power of the sea currents at the time of deposition, with each sandy layer probably being laid down quickly as a sheet. Small-scale cross-bedding confirms current activity, though clearly at

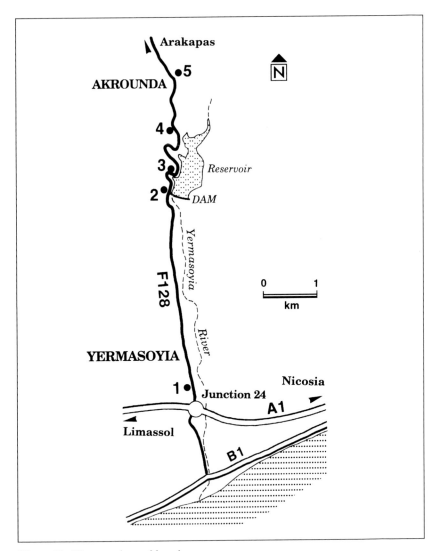

Figure 70: Yermasoyia road locations.

a diminished intensity from when the channelling occurred. The mildest
depositional activity is indicated by strongly bioturbated (organically-churned)
layers. There are several of these. One adjacent to a T-junction signpost and
about 1.5m above pavement level is 15cm thick and extends for at least 50m at

accessible level. It is full of circular tubes up to 6mm across which resemble closely the traces of *Thalassinoides* and *Planolites*. The tubes are horizontally and obliquely orientated and show as darker brown patches in a pale brown matrix.

Probably the most significant layers are those which are dominated by fragments of a creamy white limestone, sometimes in a highly comminuted state, at other times as spherical pebbles and flat plates up to 15cm in length. The best examples occur at the water fountain, where there are two such pebbly layers, the lower being 30cm thick and the upper 80cm thick. A close inspection of the pebbles, which are set in a brown Pakhna matrix, shows that they are replete with very small spherical organic components less than 0.1 mm across (they can be readily seen with a hand lens). These microfossils are probably foraminifera and algae. But the curiosity about the situation is that both the lithology and the fossils are very similar to parts of the older Lefkara Formation, which outcrops 5km to the north. The fragments are almost certainly Lefkara material and thus it is highly likely that the Lefkara chalky limestones must have been partly hardened, and then subject to intense erosion during Pakhna times, to account for the observed relationship.

While looking for all these sedimentary structures you will be able to pick out several shelly pockets and lenses, up to 30cm thick, which are full of decalcified traces of ribbed and smooth bivalves, some of *Pecten* type. Spines and other fragments of *Clypeaster*-type echinoids are also present. These organisms confirm the marine origin of the deposits.

The road now leads on to the Yermasoyia Dam some 4km (2) to the north, a dam built in 1968 and supplying water to the Limassol and Akrotiri region. Like most new major dams in Cyprus it has been constructed to withstand earthquake damage. Shallow depth earth tremors of magnitude 5-7 have been recorded within the island and offshore within recent historical times. It is located just to the south of a NE-SW trending fault, the trace of which can be seen in the cliff face above the Akrounda (Akrounta) road, about 100m north of the west end of the dam. The best viewpoint is from the centre of the dam, because this shows the change in dip of the Pakhna Formation beds on each side of the fault from gently dipping southwards to nearly horizontal. Moreover, by standing in this position you can see that the upper surface of the Pakhna in the cliff has been carved into a bowl-like depression filled with breccio-conglomerate. This is a mantle of much younger, Quaternary material deposited in a scoured-out channel when climatic conditions were much wetter than at present.

These spectacular breccio-conglomerates are beautifully exposed at the road side some 500m further along, above a narrow embayment in the reservoir (3) (076453) (Figure 71). A conveniently labelled road markerpost indicates Akrounda 3km. The cross-section through the gently dipping deposits, which are

at least 45m thick here, shows their variability: some lenticular layers consist of
large boulders up to 1m in size set in a sand matrix, some of much smaller
pebbles and yet others where large and small boulders are randomly mixed.
Although the larger pebbles tend to show some degree of rounding, the bulk are
quite angular, hence the name breccio-conglomerate. Most of the angular debris
is locally derived material from the Pakhna and Lefkara Formations. You are
looking at a small-scale example of an alluvial fan heading into the adjacent
valley and probably of Quaternary age. On the northern side of the Troodos
Range, much larger scale deposits of this age are also known as fanglomerates, a
name indicating that they were laid down as subaerial and even submarine fans
radiating from the foothills of the adjacent mountainous terrain.

Figure 71: Breccio-conglomerate fan deposits.

1.5km further on at 078458 the road swings briefly to the northwest away
from the reservoir before descending into Akrounda (Akrounta) village. At this
point on the lefthand side of the road an extensive cliff face exposes thinly
bedded Lefkara Formation chalks (4). Their distinguishing feature here,
however, is not so much the lithology but the presence of closely spaced joints,
striking in a WNW-ESE direction and dipping at a high angle (45-70°) to the
bedding, which hereabouts is 10-20° to the south (Figure 72). What you are
looking at is a type of fracture cleavage developed in the chalks (and adjacent
Pakhna beds) during powerful compressional earth movements. It is possible to
verify the lateral extent of this zone of fracturing 1km to the ESE at 086457
along the Phinikaria road, which runs above the eastern side of the reservoir. In

Figure 72: Fracture cleavage in the Lefkara Formation chalks. Notebook is 20cm long.

fact, this zone can be traced for several kilometres to the WNW and NW, to well beyond Yerasa village 13km away, and some 9km away to the SE near to Pyrgos (see p. 102). It is usually referred to as the Yerasa Fold and Fault Zone or Belt and is clearly a tectonically disturbed zone of some importance, in which the beds are often tightly folded, overturned and faulted. The main phase of earth movement which saw the development of these structures probably occurred in late Miocene times, when the Limassol Forest ophiolite mass to the north thrust southwards over and against the younger Lefkara and Pakhna Formations.

Descend the road into the southern outskirts of Akrounda noting that the steeply northwards dipping chalks abruptly cease against what is inferred to be the line of a major NW-SE thrust fault, part of the Yerasa Belt, in which the rocks to the north have been pushed up and over the chalks to the south. A few tens of metres short of the first houses there is an easily recognised patch of slipped and tumbled ground rising to the north from the roadside (5). This exposes part of the late Cretaceous (Maastrichtian) Moni Melange (see p. 102), which here has a much narrower outcrop than at Moni 11km to the east. The brown bentonitic clay, which typifies the matrix material of the melange, is sprinkled with blocks of basalt and sandstone (olistoliths), though many of these are very strongly weathered, difficult to identify and look as though they have disintegrated further during recent landslipping. This ground is very susceptible to such slips. The narrowing of the melange outcrop is caused by overthrusting of the Limassol Forest ophiolite, more especially the serpentinitised harzburgite core, southwards over the melange. Some 750m to the east of the village, a number of closely-spaced thrusts, again part of the Yerasa Belt, have cut out the pillow lavas at the top of the ophiolite sequence completely.

GLOSSARY

Acid: Term applied to igneous rocks with greater than 65 per cent silica content.

Alluvium: Deposit laid down from rivers.

Amphibolite: A metamorphic rock composed essentially of amphibole and plagioclase feldspar.

Amphibolite facies: A group of metamorphic rocks formed under moderately high pressure and temperature.

Amygdale: A gas cavity in igneous rocks infilled by secondary minerals, such as calcite and zeolites.

Andesite: An intermediate, fine grained igneous rock occurring as lava flows and containing plagioclase feldspar and hornblende.

Banding: The structure of rocks having near-parallel layers of different texture, colour or mineralogy.

Basalt: A fine grained, dark coloured volcanic rock usually occurring as lava flows and formed of plagioclase feldspar, pyroxene and iron ore. The silica percentage is usually less than 52 per cent.

Beach rock: Recent sand or pebble deposit laid down in the intertidal zone and cemented by secondary calcium carbonate, especially in warm water seas.

Bentonite: A clay rock formed by the alteration of volcanic ash and rich in smectite clay minerals.

Bioturbation: The churning of sediment by the activities of burrowing, boring and grazing organisms.

Bivalve: A mollusc in which the two valves are commonly roughly equal in size, shape and symmetry.

Boninite: A glassy high Mg basic to intermediate lava.

Breccia: A coarse grained rock formed of angular fragments. Can be deposited as a sediment or is present in fault zones.

Calcrete (Caliche): A near-surface deposit cemented by secondary calcium carbonate precipitated from evaporating groundwater. The process is known as calcretisation. Havara and kafkalla are local names.

Chert: A dense, commonly white to grey siliceous rock, usually occuring as nodules and thin seams.

Chilled margin: The border of an igneous body generally finer grained than the main mass due to more rapid cooling.

Clay: A very fine grained clastic sedimentary rock in which minute clay minerals usually are a prominent constituent. More lithified equivalents are called shales or mudrocks.

Columnar structure: A polygonal pattern of near-vertical cooling joints in basaltic rocks.

Concretion: A nodular concentration of secondary minerals precipitated within a pre-existing sediment, such as ironstone and chert nodules.

Conglomerate: A coarse grained clastic sedimentary rock formed of rounded and sub-rounded fragments.

Convolute bedding: A contortion of bedding planes and laminae in semi-lithified sediments.

Cross-stratification: A general term for layers deposited at an angle to the true bedding surfaces.

Crystallisation: The process whereby crystals separate from a fluid, a viscous or solid state.

Dacite: A quartz-bearing andesite type of lava flow.

Debris flow: A gravitational flow of sediment and fluid in which large fragments are suspended in a finer grained matrix.

Diabase: An altered dolerite in British usage.

Dolerite: A medium grained basic igneous rock composed of plagioclase feldspar, pyroxene and iron-ore.

Dunite: An essentially mono-mineralic rock composed of olivine.

Dyke: A sheet-like igneous body, usually with a near-vertical attitude. Dykes closely associated in time and space are known as a swarm.

Evaporite: A chemical sediment formed by the precipitation of salt minerals from water.

Epiclastic: A term used for weathered and eroded volcanic materials.

Epidote: A complex green silicate containing calcium, aluminium and iron found in calcium-bearing rocks which have been metamorphosed.

Extrusive rocks: Igneous rocks formed by eruption of lava onto the Earth's surface.

Facies: The total characteristics of a rock from which can be inferred the conditions of formation.

Fanglomerate: A poorly sorted conglomerate or breccia deposited in the form of an alluvial fan.

Fault breccia: A breccia formed along a fault plane.

Feeder: A dyke or pipe of igneous rock which served as a feeding channel for larger intrusive or extrusive igneous masses.

Flame structure: Curved plume of fine grained sediment fingering into an overlying coarser bed and caused by loading.

Foliation: A compositional layering in metamorphic and igneous rocks, commonly caused by a preferred orientation of minerals.

Foraminifera: Single celled and free-floating marine micro-organisms with a skeleton (test) commonly formed of calcium carbonate.

Formation: An assemblage of rocks with a characteristic lithology which allows it to be mapped.

Fracture cleavage: A series of closely spaced parallel joints produced in deformed rocks by earth pressures.

Gabbro: A coarse grained basic igneous rock consisting essentially of plagioclase feldspar and augite.

Gastropod: A snail-like one-valved mollusc in which the shells are commonly conical.

Gossan: A Cornish word for the oxidised outcrop commonly overlying iron-rich ore bodies.

Graded bedding: Shown by beds which are comparatively coarse grained at the base and which change upwards into finer grained material.

Greenstone facies: Mildly metamorphosed basic igneous rocks rich in chlorite and serpentine.

Harzburgite: An ultrabasic igneous rock rich in orthopyroxenes and olivine, both of which commonly show secondary alteration.

Hyaloclastite: A glassy volcanic tuff or ash produced by rapid cooling and fragmentation of lava erupted into water.

Inlier: An outcrop of rocks totally surrounded by younger rocks.

Limestone: A sedimentary rock composed dominantly of organic and inorganic calcite (calcium carbonate).

Lithification: The process of hardening, induration and compaction of sediments leading to the formation of solid rocks.

Load cast: Sedimentary structure where rounded downwards-protrusions of coarse material have sunk vertically into finer material below.

Magma: The molten fluid generated within the earth and from which igneous rocks are derived.

Mantle: The zone of the geosphere situated at a depth of about 35km below the crust and extending inwards to the core, about 2900km distant. It is generally assumed to be ultrabasic in composition (peridotite). Harzburgite is a modified variety of peridotite.

Marble: Metamorphosed limestone.

Marl: A sediment formed of a mixture of calcite and clay.

Massive: A term commonly used to describe sedimentary beds which are uniform in texture from top to bottom. They need not necessarily be thick beds.

Melange: A mixed sedimentary deposit of variably sized blocks of mixed lithology incorporated in a clay matrix, which may be sheared. Often caused initially by submarine sliding but may then be affected by powerful earth stresses (see olistostrome).

Member: Part of a formation, recognised by some individual lithological peculiarity.

Mineralisation: The impregnation of rock with minerals, some of which might be of economic importance.

Obduction: The process of displacement of a plate so that it moves into a position above an adjacent plate.

Ochre: An iron oxide- and manganese oxide-rich pigment commonly formed during the weathering of pyritic ore-bodies.

Olistolith: An exotic block of rock brought into place by slipping and sliding.

Olistostrome: A sedimentary formation, commonly submarine, made up of a chaotic assemblage of blocks of mixed lithology set in a clay matrix.

Ophiolite: An assemblage of ultrabasic and basic igneous rocks, commonly generated along the constructive margins between spreading plates.

Pegmatite: A coarse grained facies of any plutonic igneous rock.

Peridotite: A coarse grained ultrabasic rock composed mainly of olivine. Feldspar is absent.

Picrite-basalt: An olivine-enriched basalt, containing phenocrysts of olivine and augite.

Pillow lava: Lava resembling a jumbled heap of pillows.

Plagiogranite: An orthoclase feldspar-free coarse granitoid rock, rich in plagioclase feldspar.

Plate: Relatively thin, being of the order of 100km thick, internally rigid blocks of continental or oceanic material forming the earth's crust. They are driven continuously across an underlying weaker asthenosphere probably by mantle convection currents.

Plate tectonics: A unifying theory for explaining the evolution of the Earth's surface, based on the movement of relatively thin, internally rigid lithospheric plates.

Plutonic: Term applied to igneous rocks formed at great depths.

Porphyritic texture: A texture of igneous rocks in which relatively large crystals (phenocrysts) are set within a finer grained matrix.

Pumice: A light coloured variety of highly porous, acid intermediate igneous lava.

Pyroxenite: A coarse grained igneous composed mainly of pyroxene.

Radiolaria: Free-floating, marine siliceous micro-organisms with a porous skeleton that easily disintegrates on death.

Radiolarian chert: A hard and brittle siliceous rock composed mainly of the disintegrated skeletons of radiolaria.

Raised Beach: Also known as a marine terrace. A deposit of sand, gravel and shell material, originally laid down at the edge of the sea, but now elevated as a consequence of a relative fall in sea-level.

Reef: A limestone formed of organisms capable of building up a rigid structure from the sea floor.

Rift faulting: Faulting along parallel lines, which produces steep-sided flat bottomed valleys, known as rift valleys or graben.

Salt deposits: Mineral salts, such as gypsum and halite, deposited through the evaporation of salt lakes or lagoons.

Sandstone: A clastic medium grained sedimentary rock usually consisting of abundant quartz intermingled with a range of other constituents, such as feldspars, micas, fossil remains and cementing agents.

Schist: A metamophic rock, the foliated structure of which is caused by the prevalence of flaky or elongated minerals.

Sea-floor spreading: The symmetrical displacement of adjacent plates by the addition of crustal material in the zone (or ridge) between them. Successive additions cause the older material to move sideways in a direction at right angles to the zone.

Serpentine: A hydrous magnesium silicate group of minerals and dominant in the rock serpentinite.

Serpentinite: A rock formed by the hydrothermal alteration of ultrabasic rocks, such as harzburgite and dunite.

Shard: An angular fragment of volcanic glass, commonly found in glassy tuffs and ashes (hyaloclastites).

Sheet flow: The movement of a dense sediment-water mix down bottom slopes.

Slump deposits: A bed of sediment internally deformed by sliding.

Smectite: A group of clay minerals with swelling properties, more especially the variety montmorillonite.

Stockwork: A mass of rock, often roughly cylindrical, which has been highly fractured and along which mineralisation has occurred.

Strike: The direction of a horizontal line drawn at right angles to the dip of the beds.

Strike-slip fault: A fault in which the rocks on each side move virtually horizontally past each other.

Stromatolite: A laminated structure formed by calcareous algae living in shallow waters.

Subduction: A process where ocean floor is destroyed by one lithospheric plate overriding another. The overriden plate is pushed down into the mantle.

Terra rossa: A red ferruginous clay found in soil profiles in southern Europe and formed by the in-place weathering of limestones.

Thrust fault: A low angle plane of dislocation caused by the near-horizontal displacement of rock masses.

Trace fossils: Structures preserved in sediments caused by the activities of burrowing, grazing and boring organisms.

Trachyte: A fine to medium grained rock, often porphyritic, and composed mainly of alkali feldspars, biotite and augite, which are commonly flow-aligned.

Transform fault: A major dislocation within the Earth's oceanic crust with a strike-slip displacement at right-angles to the axes of spreading plates.

Tuff: An indurated pyroclastic rock formed of volcanic ash fragments.

Turbidity current: A cloud of highly mobile suspended sediment which commonly moves with considerable velocity down bottom slopes. The sedimentary product is known as a turbidite.

Ultrabasic: A term describing igneous rocks with a low silica content, such as dunite, and composed of an abundance of ferro-magnesian silicates.

Umber: A very fine grained iron oxide- and manganese oxide-rich sediment, associated with basic lava flows.

Unconformity: A structural feature separating two sets of strata and representing, usually, a considerable time break. Sometimes there is an angular discordance between the sets.

Vesicle: A small oval or irregular cavity in an igneous rock produced by escaping gas.

Volcaniclastic rocks: Sediments composed of mechanically transported material of volcanic origin.

Volcaniclastic sandstone: A sediment of sand grade formed predominantly or material originally ejected from volcanic vents. Usually contains traces of volcanic glass and pumice.

Wehrlite: An ultrabasic igneous rock composed of olivines, pyroxenes, hornblende and iron-ores.

Zeolite facies: Rocks showing low grade metamorphism and characterised by the presence of zeolites.

Zeolites: Hydrated silicates of calcium and aluminium, sometimes with sodium and aluminium. They include analcite (a cubic form) and heulandite.

FURTHER READING

The literature on Cyprus geology is immense, in several languages, and is not always readily accessible. The Cyprus Geological Survey Department has produced many detailed Memoirs over recent decades and their availability can be checked with the Department of Lands and Surveys in Nicosia. The selection below has proved most useful in the compilation of this Guide:

BOYLE, J.F & ROBERTSON, A.H.F. 1984. Evolving metallogenesis at the Troodos spreading axis. In: *Ophiolites and Oceanic Lithosphere* (I.G. Gass, S.J. Lippard & A.W. Shelton; eds). Geol. Soc. Spec. Publ. No. 13, 169-81.

CASEY, J.F. & DEWEY, J.F. 1984. Initiation of subduction zones along transform and accreting plate boundaries, triple-junction evolution, and forearc spreading centres — implications for ophiolite geology and obduction. In: *Ophiolites and Oceanic Lithosphere* (I.G. Gass, S.J. Lippard & A.W. Shelton; eds.). Geol. Soc. Spec. Publ. No. 13, 269-290.

CONSTANTINOU, G. & GOVETT, G.J.S.,1972. Genesis of sulphide deposits, ochre and umber of Cyprus. *Trans. Inst. Mining & Metallurgy*, Section B, **81**, B34-B46.

CONSTANTINOU, G. & GOVETT, G.J.S. 1973. Geology, geochemistry and genesis of Cyprus sulphide deposits. *Economic Geol.*, **68**, 843-58.

CYPRUS TOURISM ORGANISATION. 1992. *Nature Trails of the Akamas.*

DUBIN, M. 1993. CYPRUS. The ROUGH GUIDE. Rough Guides Ltd, London.

FARRELL, S.G. & EATON S. 1987. Slump strain in the Tertiary of Cyprus and the Spanish Pyrenees. Definition of palaeoslopes and models of soft-sediment deformation. In: *Deformation of Sediments and Sedimentary Rocks.* (Jones, M.E. & R.M.F. Preston; eds) Geol. Soc. Spec. Publ. No. 29, 181-96.

GASS, I.G. & MASSON-SMITH, D. 1963. The geology and gravity anomalies of the Troodos Massif, Cyprus. *Phil. Trans. Roy. Soc. London.*, series A, **255**, 417-67.

GASS, I.G. & SMEWING, J.D. 1973. Intrusion, Extrusion and Metamorphism at Constructive Margins: Evidence from the Troodos Massif, Cyprus. *Nature, Lond.*, **242**, 26-9.

GASS, I.G. 1989. Magmatic processes at and near constructive plate margins as deduced from the Troodos (Cyprus) and Semail Nappe (N. Oman) ophiolites. In: *Magmatism in the Ocean Basins.* (Saunders, A.D. & M.J. Norry; eds) Geol. Soc. Spec. Publ. No. 42, 1-15.

GREENBAUM, D. 1977. The Chromitiferous Rocks of the Troodos Ophiolite Complex, Cyprus. *Economic Geol.*, **72**, 1175-94.

HUNT, D. (ed). 1982. *Footprints in Cyprus*. Trigraph, London.

MOORES, E.M. & VINE, F.J. 1971. The Troodos Massif, Cyprus and other ophiolites as oceanic crust: evaluation and implications. *Phil. Trans. Roy. Soc. Lond.*, series A, **268**, 443-66.

OPEN UNIVERSITY. 1991 *The Ocean Basins: their Structure and Evolution*. Pergamon Press, Oxford.

OXBURGH, E.R. 1974. *The Plain Man's Guide to Plate tectonics*. Proc. Geologists' Assoc., **85**, 299-357.

PALMER, T. 1990 *Discover Cyprus and North Cyprus*. Heritage House, Clacton-on-Sea.

POOLE, A.J., SHIMMIELD, G.B. & ROBERTSON, A.H.F. 1990 Late Quaternary uplift of the Troodos ophiolite, Cyprus: Uranium-series dating of Pleistocene coral. *Geology*, **18**, 894-97.

ROBERTSON, A.H.F. & HUDSON J.D. 1974. Pelagic sediments in the Cretaceous and Tertiary history of the Troodos Massif, Cyprus. *Spec. Publ. Int. Ass. Sediment.*, **1**, 406-36.

ROBERTSON, A.H.F. 1976. Pelagic chalks and calciturbidites from the Lower Tertiary of the Troodos Massif, Cyprus. *J. Sedimentary Petrol.*, **46**, 1007-16.

ROBERTSON, A.H.F. 1977. Tertiary uplift of the Troodos Massif, Cyprus. *Geol. Soc. America Bull.*, **88**, 1763-72.

ROBERTSON A.H.F. 1977. The Moni Melange, Cyprus: an olistostrome formed at a destructive plate margin. *Jl. Geol. Soc. Lond.*, **133**, 447-66.

ROBERTSON A.H.F. 1977.The Kannaviou Formation, Cyprus: volcaniclastic sedimentation of a probable late Cretaceous volcanic arc. *Jl. Geol. Soc. Lond.*, **134**, 269-92.

ROBERTSON A.H.F. & WOODCOCK, N.H. 1979. The Mamonia Complex, southwest Cyprus: the evolution and emplacement of a Mesozoic continental margin. *Geol. Soc. America Bull.*, **90**, 651-665.

ROBERTSON, A.H.F. & WOODCOCK, N.H. 1980 Tectonic setting of the Troodos massif in the eastern Mediterranean. In: *Ophiolites*. Proc. Internat. Ophiolite Symposium, Cyprus 1979, 36-49.

SCHMINCKE, H.U., RAUTENSCHLEIN, M., ROBINSON, P.T. &
    MEHEGAN, J.M. 1983. Troodos extrusive series of Cyprus: A comparison
    with oceanic crust. *Geology*, **11**, 405-9.

SIMONIAN, K.O. & GASS, I.G. 1978. The Arakapas fault belt, Cyprus: a fossil
    transform fault. *Geol. Soc. America Bull.*, **89**, 1220-30.

SWARBRICK, R.E. & NAYLOR, M.A. 1980. The Kathikas melange, SW
    Cyprus: late Cretaceous submarine debris flows. *Sedimentology*, **27**, 63-78.

THUBRON, C. 1986. *Journey into Cyprus.* Penguin.

VARGA, R.J. & MOORES, E.M. 1985. Spreading structure of the Troodos
    ophiolite, Cyprus. *Geology*, **13**, 846-50.